MELBOURNE
A CITY OF STORIES

MELBOURNE
A CITY OF STORIES

EDITED BY
DEBORAH TOUT-SMITH

CONTRIBUTING AUTHORS
REBECCA CARLAND
MATTHEW CHURCHWARD
DAVID CROTTY
LIZA DALE-HALLETT
DAVID DEMANT
RICHARD GILLESPIE
FIONA KINSEY
MOYA MCFADZEAN
MICHAEL REASON
ADRIAN REGAN
SARAH ROOD
ANTOINETTE SMITH
CHARLOTTE SMITH
DEBORAH TOUT-SMITH
NURIN VEIS
ELIZABETH WILLIS

MUSEUMVICTORIA

Published by Museum Victoria 2008
Reprinted 2009

Museum Victoria
GPO Box 666
Melbourne VIC 3001 Australia
Telephone: + 61 3 8341 7777
www.museumvictoria.com.au

Dr J Patrick Greene
CHIEF EXECUTIVE OFFICER

Dr Robin Hirst
DIRECTOR, COLLECTIONS, RESEARCH AND EXHIBITIONS

Dr Richard Gillespie
HEAD, HISTORY AND TECHNOLOGY DEPARTMENT

DESIGN
Toni Jolic for Design Consortium

National Library of Australia
Cataloguing-in-Publication entry:

Author: Tout-Smith, Deborah.
Title: Melbourne: a city of stories / edited by Deborah Tout-Smith.
Publisher: Melbourne: Museum Victoria, 2008.
Edition: Rev. ed.

ISBN: 9780980381375 (pbk.)
Notes: Includes index.
             Bibliography.
Subjects: Museum Victoria–Exhibitions.
             Melbourne (Vic.)–History–Exhibitions.
             Melbourne (Vic.)–Social life and customs–Exhibitions.
             Melbourne (Vic.)–Exhibitions.
Other Authors/Contributors: Tout-Smith, Deborah.
             Museum Victoria.

Dewey Number: 994.51

Cover image: **Bourke Street, Melbourne, early 1900s,** Source – Alexander Turnbull Library, New Zealand
Page ii image: **Elizabeth Street, Melbourne, looking north from Flinders Street, late 1800s,** Source – State Library of Victoria

CONTENTS

FOREWORD

Melbourne: a city of stories grew out of Melbourne Museum's long-term exhibition, *The Melbourne Story*. That makes it a selective history: one based on objects – things that have survived. The idea that objects can give rise to stories comes as no surprise to anyone who's ever dug up a shard of old china in their garden, or found an ancient button down the back of a chair. 'I wonder what its story is,' you think. And the wondering can sometimes be more thrilling than the finding out – but not always.

As a volunteer on the first 'Little Lon' archaeological excavation, in 1988, I had whole months crammed with discovery and wondering. Bones and bottles, clay pipes and coins, pins and pickle jars: all kinds of things emerged from the dirt of a Melbourne city block. It was a waste ground, a building site in waiting; but somebody – plenty of somebodies – must have lived and worked there and left all this stuff behind. I'd seen old maps of the area, showing cottages and workshops crowded together along narrow lanes. But the people who'd inhabited them and who'd thrown away or lost the objects we dug up – their names and lives were a mystery to me.

The artefacts from the Little Lon excavations now form part of Museum Victoria's collection. A selection of them features in both *The Story of Melbourne* exhibition and in this book, together with stories that shed light on the lives of those who left them behind. It's as if the objects have been given a voice. Still, though, there's room left for wondering. How did that teacup get broken? Questions like that cry out for a story.

And what about all the things from Melbourne's past that haven't survived? It's largely a matter of chance as to what's preserved and what's thrown out or pulled down. Take, for instance, Melbourne's first newspaper, the *Melbourne Advertiser*, founded by John Pascoe Fawkner in 1838. Copies of the newspaper survive, as does the press on which it was printed (p. 16). But the building that housed the press and the cobbled laneway in which that building stood are long gone.

The eastern end of Melbourne, 1858
Part of a panorama depicting Melbourne from Flagstaff Hill
Lithographer – George Rowe. Source – State Library of Victoria

Always, I find, I'm drawn to absences, the stories untold. Even when an object survives, those echoes remain. Whether it's an Aboriginal canoe from the Yarra River or a US secret service agent's paint-spattered shirt, the objects tantalise, seeming to pose as many questions as they give away answers.

Melbourne: a city of stories reflects on both the place and its people, telling not just the big story but small ones as well. Against the blare of Marvellous Melbourne, William Barak speaks up for the rights of Aborigines. Melbourne becomes the nation's capital and William Douglas is admitted to the Kew Asylum. And as the city leaps into the electric age, the Hecla brand of appliances is born in a garden shed.

This book, like the exhibition on which it is based, draws the reader into a sense of exploring the city's layers through time. Its emphasis is less on the proud public record than on objects and people with stories to tell and a place in Melbourne's history.

History well told is less like a photo album – jumping snapshot to snapshot, from one fact to the next – than it is like a movie, the facts threaded together and set in motion to tell a story. Or stories. That's what this book does.

Robyn Annear

The streets of Little Lon, early 1870s

Source – State Library of New South Wales

MELBOURNE, THE MEETING PLACE   1835–1850

On an early winter's day in 1835, alongside a beautiful stream, a group of Aboriginal men gathered around a bearded stranger.

His name was John Batman. He hoped to become fabulously rich – by buying 500 000 acres of Aboriginal land in exchange for a few household goods.

This transaction – meaningless to the Aborigines that day and immediately rejected by government – marked the foundation of Melbourne.

KEY DATES

Before settlement, thousands of Aboriginal people live in the Port Phillip region

1803 Convict settlement established at Sorrento, led by Lieutenant-Colonel David Collins, but soon abandoned due to lack of water, poor soil and unsuitability as a port

1835 First permanent European settlement established on the site of Melbourne

1837 Melbourne is named after Lord Melbourne, the British prime minister

1837 Surveyor Robert Hoddle lays out Melbourne's central grid of streets

1839 First shipload of immigrants arrives from Britain

1842 First flour mills and iron foundry are established

1843 First election – landholders elect Port Phillip District representatives for the New South Wales Legislative Council

1847 Melbourne town is raised to the status of a city by the authority of Queen Victoria

1850 Royal assent to the separation of the Port Phillip District from New South Wales; Victoria becomes a self-governing colony

1850 Melbourne's population: 20 500

Nº 1. J. Batman Esqr.
    2. Mount Macedon.
    3. Surveyors Office.
    4. A. Kemmis & Cos Stores.
    5. Barracks & Gaol.
    6. ___ Carrington Esqr.
    7. Marshalls Emigration Office.
    8. Strughan & Cos Stores.
    9. Melbourne Auction Rooms.
    10. Police Office.

MELBO

Clark & Cº Colonial Booksellers

11. Lamb Inn.
12. The Basin of the Yarra Yarra.
13. Melbourne Club House.
14. Flinder Street.
15. W. Le Souef Esqʳ J.P.
16. Elizabeth Street.
17. Custom House.
18. Swanston Street.
19. Russell Street.
20. East Hill.

URNE.

Phillip.)

Melbourne has always been a meeting place.

Aboriginal people of the Kulin nation gathered every year near the Yarra River for ceremonies, celebrations and trade. These were important social gatherings where political and family alliances were reinforced and grievances addressed.

They camped in clearings and on hills: on the future site of the Melbourne Cricket Ground, on the hill where Government House now stands and along the Yarra at Burnley and Clifton Hill. The area offered plentiful food sources from several rivers, the bay, the hills and the plains.

These landscapes had been formed over millions of years. In the east and north-east, ancient sediments were warped into hills and valleys. In the south and south-east, later coastal sediments were laid down to form a broad plain. To the west and north, lava spread out to create a volcanic plain.

Port Phillip Bay is a recent arrival. It was formed about 10 000 years ago, when sea levels rose at the end of the last Ice Age. Until then, the Yarra River flowed along a valley in what is now the eastern side of the bay.

Melbourne, 1839
When this picture was painted, Melbourne was already an established town with a population of almost 3000, mostly clustered on the higher northern bank of the Yarra River.
Artist – John Adamson. Source – State Library of Victoria

13

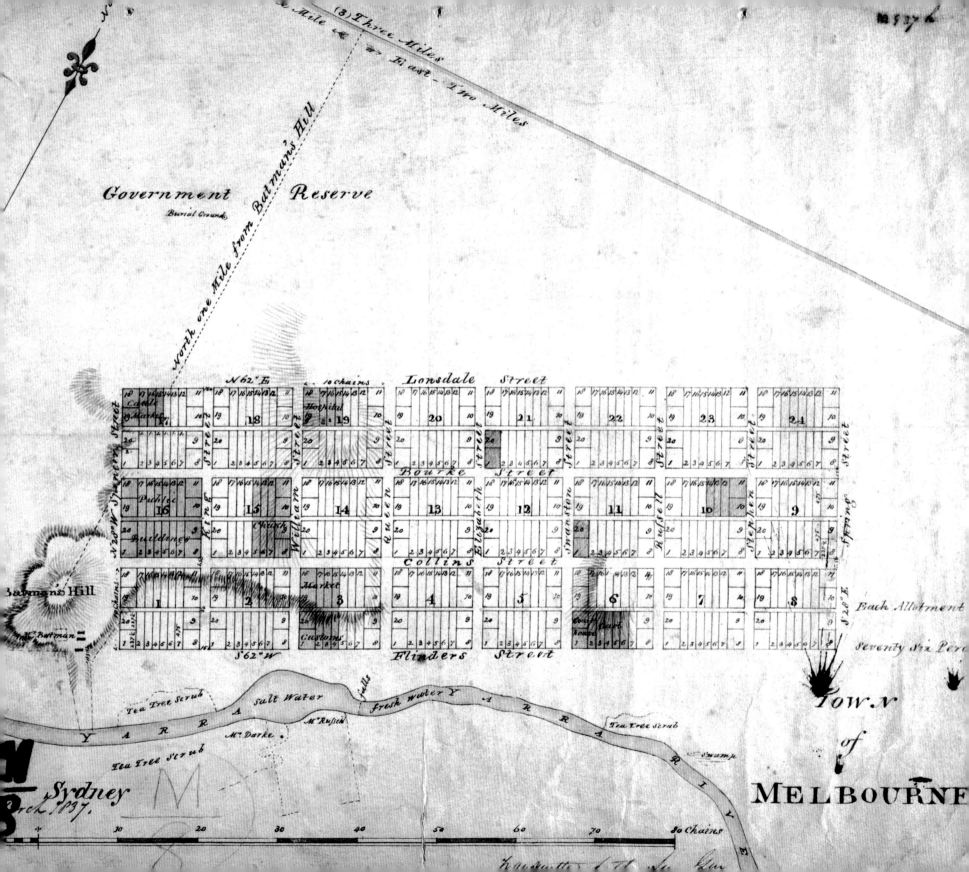

Government Reserve

Burial Ground

North one Mile from Batmans Hill

(3) Three Miles
East Two Miles

Lonsdale Street

Bourke Street

Collins Street

Flinders Street

Batman's Hill

Mr Batman

Mr Russel
Mr Darke
Salt Water
Fresh Water
Tea Tree Scrub
Tea Tree Scrub

Y A R R A   R I V E R

TOWN
of
MELBOURNE

Each Allotment
Seventy Six Per

Sydney
1837.

10   20   30   40   50   60   70   80 Chains

Aboriginal people fishing at night on Merri Creek, 1864

Artist – François Cogné. Source – Alexander Turnbull Library, New Zealand

Town of Melbourne, **March 1837**

The beginnings of Melbourne's central street grid are visible in this plan, prepared by Robert Hoddle for the first government land sales.

Source – Public Record Office Victoria

Into this fertile landscape came European settlers, attracted by the rich pastures to the west and north of Port Phillip. The charge was led by businessmen from Van Dieman's Land (Tasmania), including John Batman, his partner John Wedge and rival John Pascoe Fawkner. They arrived in June 1835 and selected a site by the Yarra River, where a ledge of basalt rock across the Yarra's bed prevented salt flowing up the river, ensuring fresh water.

The government of New South Wales tried to stop the settlement. In August 1835, all settlers were pronounced trespassers and a deed that Batman had struck with the Kulin for land was declared void. But news of the settlement at Port Phillip had already spread. More ships were crossing Bass Strait from Van Diemen's Land and dropping anchor in the Yarra River. Young men, eager for opportunity and adventure, disembarked in increasing numbers, sometimes bringing with them women and children and herds of animals. The bush was trampled and cleared further every day, and the clusters of settlers' tents grew. By June 1836, the settlement boasted 177 settlers living in a scattering of buildings, turf huts and tents, and more than 26 000 sheep.

The New South Wales government accepted the inevitable and hastened to establish control, sending Captain William Lonsdale to take charge of law and order in September 1836. Soon the tools of authority were in place, including a courthouse and police lock-up. In March 1837, Governor Sir Richard Bourke proclaimed Melbourne a town during his brief visit from Sydney. Its name was chosen to flatter the prime minister of Great Britain, Lord Melbourne.

Robert Hoddle, the senior surveyor for New South Wales, began pegging out allotments so land sales could begin. Arriving in Melbourne with Governor Bourke's party, he had less than a month to make a survey in preparation for government land sales. Hoddle gave central Melbourne its distinctive grid of streets. The grid pattern followed standard surveying regulations of the period, but Hoddle determined its alignment – tilted slightly from the usual north–south orientation, so the main streets would run parallel to the Yarra River. He also made Melbourne's main streets unusually wide, 'on the score of health, and convenience for the future city'. The narrow intervening laneways were Governor Bourke's idea.

PRINTING MELBOURNE'S FIRST NEWSPAPER

John Pascoe Fawkner, 1792–1869

The first newspaper in Melbourne, the *Melbourne Advertiser*, was printed in 1838 on this 18th-century English Common Press, brought to Melbourne by John Pascoe Fawkner.

The son of an English convict, Fawkner had left Van Diemen's Land determined to help create a fairer society at Port Phillip. He even drafted an idealistic constitution for the new settlement. But he was equally determined to make money.

Fawkner used the press until 1840 and it was later used to print the *Geelong Advertiser*. It became one of the founding objects of the Industrial and Technological Museum, which opened in 1870.

Fawkner's press

Photographer – Jon Augier. Source – Museum Victoria

Batman's Hill and House on the Yarra
In 1863, Liardet sketched Batman's house from memory,
as it would have appeared in the late 1830s.

Artist – W F E Liardet. Source – National Library of Australia

Perched atop a tree stump, Hoddle acted as auctioneer at Melbourne's first land sale on 1 June 1837. The 100 half-acre allotments – the city's heart – sold for an average £38 each.

By the end of the year around 100 houses were standing, but most settlers still lived in tents or in rough huts of wattle and daub (clay) on tea-tree frames, roofed with bark or shingles. Roads were boggy tracks, food supplies were uncertain and water from the Yarra River tasted muddy. Basic services such as hospitals and schools were lacking. Public disorder and drunkards were ever threatening.

More substantial homes and public buildings soon began to appear on the landscape. Settlers continued to arrive, and by 1838 more than 3500 were living in the Melbourne area. In that year, too, Melbourne reached a milestone: its first newspaper was published. John Pascoe Fawkner founded the *Melbourne Advertiser* to throw 'the resplendent light of Publicity upon all the affairs of this New Colony'. It was full of advertisements: goods for sale, livestock lost and found, and servants wanted. It also listed shipping arrivals and cargoes, and named those caught drunk or fighting, or riding their horses too fast.

The earliest editions of the *Melbourne Advertiser* were handwritten. Fawkner had ordered a printing press but couldn't wait for it to arrive – he wanted the glory of being first to publish. His old wooden press arrived in Melbourne weeks later and was quickly set to work. But after just seven weeks Fawkner was forced to stop publishing because he lacked a licence, and it took almost a year for him to publish Melbourne's next newspaper.

Meanwhile, other presses were also printing stories of Melbourne. In Britain, newspapers and pamphlets began to talk admiringly of Melbourne's progress and to encourage emigration to the small town with great pretensions at the bottom of the Australian mainland:

> *Melbourne is a handsome town, numbering more than 3,000 inhabitants … Lying to the south of Sydney and the older settlements, its climate and resources are superior …*
>
> *[The Australian colonies are] calling for tens of thousands of reapers of sobriety and ability, to come and exchange privation for abundance, penury and dependence for smiling plenty, and every enjoyment a reasonable man can desire.*

(*Emigration – Its Necessity and Advantages*, 1840)

MELBOURNE'S COAT OF ARMS

This cast-iron coat of arms came from the Eastern Market, once located at the corner of Bourke and Exhibition Streets. The market was founded in 1847 and demolished in 1960.

The coat of arms design reflects much about early Melbourne. The St George's cross and royal crown declare the town's allegiance to Great Britain. The sheep, bull and whale represent the colony's chief exports in 1842 – wool, tallow, hides and whale oil – and the ship depicts the settlement's means of communication with the outside world.

Melbourne's coat of arms

Photographer – Rodney Start. Source – Museum Victoria

Collins Street, town of Melbourne, New South Wales, 1839
Artist – William Knight. Source – National Library of Australia

Settlers responded to the call in increasing numbers. Most came to Melbourne seeking opportunity: to get rich, to improve their social status, to build a new life or to escape an old one. The first British migrant ship to sail direct to Melbourne was the *David Clarke*, arriving from Scotland in October 1839. Other settlers came on coastal vessels from Van Diemen's Land. A few dared the overland journey through the bush from Sydney. In the chaos of the fast-growing settlement ex-convicts rubbed shoulders with free settlers and young aristocrats, all eager for opportunity and adventure.

Officially, Melbourne wasn't a convict settlement. But during the 1840s Port Phillip accepted ex-convicts from Van Dieman's Land and shipments of convicts with conditional pardons from Britain. They laboured on public works, in spite of opposition from the new Melbourne Town Council; others were sent to work on pastoral properties beyond Melbourne. By 1850, within 15 years of settlement, about one-quarter of the men in Port Phillip were ex-convicts.

Then in 1842, after years of optimism and growth, the town's progress faltered. Wool and tallow (animal fat) prices fell, land values and investments collapsed and the economy sank into depression. Hundreds of Melburnians became bankrupt and the poor and unemployed were left to struggle for themselves. It would take several years for Melbourne to regain its footing.

The European settlement was far more of a disaster for the Kulin people. The government began distributing the land around Melbourne on the assumption that it belonged to the Crown. Aborigines were forced from their lands and deprived of their traditional sources of food; some bartered goods or sold firewood to survive. They also faced deadly diseases such as dysentery and smallpox. Assistant Protector William Thomas reported that within 20 years of Melbourne's settlement the numbers of Woi wurrung and Boon wurrung in the area had fallen to only 28 people.

PUNT ACROSS THE YARRA RIVER

Without a bridge, the Yarra posed a challenge to settlers wanting to get their goods and livestock across the river.

Joseph Stevenson, a Scottish-born carpenter, built Melbourne's first punt using old ship timbers and hand tools. Christened *The Melbourne* with a bottle of imported champagne, the punt was launched on Easter Sunday 1838. It was operated by publican Thomas Watt.

When a second punt posed competition, Watt offered his passengers free beer. Brickmakers from the south side of the Yarra kept crossing the river until they were drunk, causing an 'outbreak against the quiet of the town', and Watt lost his punt licence.

Punts became redundant after a wooden toll bridge opened in 1845. Five years later it was replaced by a single-arched stone structure, the original Princes Bridge.

Punt on the Yarra, Melbourne, about 1840

Artist – Charles Norton. Engraver – Ham Brothers. Source – State Library of Victoria

Tools used to build Melbourne's first punt

Photographer – Rodney Start. Source – Museum Victoria

A COLONIST APPRECIATED

William Westgarth, 1815–1889

When William Westgarth returned to Britain on business in 1847, some 120 fellow colonists presented him with this gift of silverware in appreciation of his services to the colony. It was made in Edinburgh by J Mckay.

In the seven years since his arrival in Melbourne, Westgarth had become a leading merchant and businessman, active in the Benevolent Society and Mechanics' Institute, and had written a book publicising the colony's potential.

Westgarth returned to Melbourne in 1849 and went on to play a prominent part in the civic life and affairs of Port Phillip, including sitting in Victoria's first parliament and helping to establish the Melbourne Chamber of Commerce.

William Westgarth later in life

Source – State Library of Queensland

William Westgarth's silverware

Photographer – Rodney Start. Source – Museum Victoria

THE YARRA CANOE

This is the only remaining 19th-century Aboriginal canoe from the Melbourne region. Scottish immigrant John Buchan collected the canoe in the 1850s from local Aborigines camping near his home overlooking the Yarra River at Studley Park, five kilometres east of central Melbourne.

The river flats and lagoons of the Yarra River were favoured places for the Woi wurrung people, providing a plentiful supply of fish, eel and birds' eggs.

The canoe is made from the bark of Mountain Ash, which grew in the ranges near Melbourne. Sharp marks show that the bark was cut with a metal rather than with a traditional stone axe. Charcoal marks suggest that the bark was heated to help shape it into a canoe.

Aboriginal people fishing from a canoe, about 1845

This watercolour sketch is of the Murray River, 250 kilometres north of Melbourne, but similar scenes occurred along the Yarra River.

Artist – Samuel Thomas Gill. Source – State Library of New South Wales

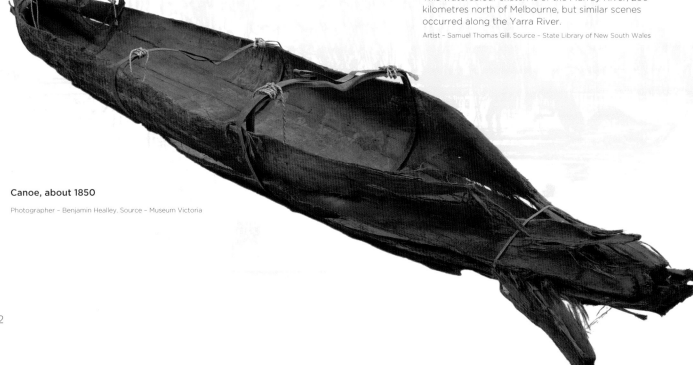

Canoe, about 1850

Photographer – Benjamin Healley. Source – Museum Victoria

THE POSSIBILITY OF COEXISTENCE

Billibellary, unknown–1846
William Thomas, 1793–1867

Billibellary was *Ngurungaeta*, the senior man of the Wurundjeri willam clan of the Woi wurrung. To the settlers he was Chief of the Yarra Tribe. He was a spokesperson for his people in negotiations with the colonial government, and he helped choose the site of the Merri Creek Station as a suitable reserve for his people.

Billibellary worked with William Thomas, the government's Assistant Protector of Aborigines, to find a way for settlers and Aboriginal people to coexist. Despite different motives, the two men encouraged the young to attend a school by the Merri Creek, established by the Baptist Church in 1846. They also tried to ensure that the Native Police, created to bring the Aborigines under British laws, acted as a force for conciliation rather than oppression.

But Billibellary died in 1846, and Thomas found it impossible to protect Aboriginal people from the dramatic changes taking place on their traditional lands.

Sketch of Billibellary in William Thomas's notebook

Artist – William Thomas. Source – State Library of Victoria

William Thomas in 1841, aged 48

Artist – G H Haydon. Source – State Library of Victoria

GOLD TOWN 1850–1880

It was June 1851. Melbourne was bubbling with anticipation: a reward for gold was being offered and rumours of finds were spreading. Melburnians turned to their own backyards and parks with spades and shovels, knives and forks. Collingwood Flat and the Flagstaff, Studley Park and Emerald Hill all rang to the sound of digging. Even a flowerpot made from glittering clay drew an excited crowd.

Gold was soon found in central Victoria, not Melbourne. Even so, the gold rush sparked the biggest boom in the city's history.

KEY DATES

1850 MELBOURNE'S POPULATION: 20 500

1851 SEPARATION OF VICTORIA FROM NEW SOUTH WALES

1851 GOLD RUSH BEGINS; IN 10 YEARS, MORE THAN HALF A MILLION PEOPLE ARRIVE IN VICTORIA

1854 NATIONAL MUSEUM OF VICTORIA, PUBLIC LIBRARY AND UNIVERSITY OF MELBOURNE ARE FOUNDED

1854 FIRST RAILWAY AND TELEGRAPH SERVICES ARE ESTABLISHED

1855 VICTORIA PASSES AUSTRALIA'S FIRST IMMIGRATION ACT, RESTRICTING CHINESE IMMIGRATION

1856 BUILDING WORKERS WIN AN EIGHT-HOUR DAY

1859 SEVEN MEMBERS OF THE MELBOURNE CRICKET CLUB CODIFY AUSTRALIAN RULES FOOTBALL, MAKING IT THE OLDEST FOOTBALL CODE IN THE WORLD

1860 BURKE AND WILLS LEAVE ON THEIR ILL-FATED EXPEDITION TO TRAVEL ACROSS THE AUSTRALIAN CONTINENT

1860 *NICHOLSON LAND ACT* AIMS TO FREE UP RURAL LAND FOR SMALLHOLDERS AND LIMIT OWNERSHIP BY WEALTHY SQUATTERS

1863 CORANDERRK ABORIGINAL STATION IS ESTABLISHED NEAR HEALESVILLE FOR THE RE-SETTLEMENT OF ABORIGINAL PEOPLE

1870 BRITAIN WITHDRAWS ITS MILITARY FORCES, LEAVING VICTORIA RESPONSIBLE FOR ITS OWN DEFENCE

1872 *VICTORIAN EDUCATION ACT* ESTABLISHES FREE, COMPULSORY AND SECULAR EDUCATION

1880 MELBOURNE'S POPULATION: 281 000

Emigrants landing at the Queens Wharf, Melbourne
Published in the *Australian News for Home Readers*, 1863.
Passengers and luggage were transferred by small paddle-
steamers from larger ships anchored in Hobsons Bay.
Artist – Nicholas Chevalier. Source – National Library of Australia

Before Victoria took its current name it was called the Port Phillip District, encompassing both Melbourne and the lands beyond. And it was part of New South Wales for 16 years.

The news that the British government had approved Victoria's separation was received with great enthusiasm on 11 November 1850. Celebrations included fireworks, street parades, games and thanksgivings. Victoria officially became a separate colony on 1 July 1851.

But something else was happening at the same time, something that gave the citizens of Melbourne cause for even more excitement: rumours that gold had been found in Victoria. A reward had been offered for the first authenticated discovery, partly as an attempt to stem the tide of hopefuls heading for the newly announced goldfields in New South Wales. Less than one month later, in July 1851, the discovery of gold in Clunes, Central Victoria, was announced. Within a short time Melbourne's ports and roadways were crowded with diggers, and in the space of just 10 years more than half a million people arrived in Melbourne. The colony of Victoria was overwhelmed.

With workers abandoning their jobs for the diggings, labour shortages caused wages to treble and crops to go unharvested. Scarcity of supplies made prices soar.

Amid the chaos of the gold rush, Victoria's inexperienced new government struggled to impose order. Governor La Trobe sent urgent pleas to London for more soldiers, and asked for warships to protect Melbourne and its gold. Hundreds of police were recruited to keep order in Melbourne and on the goldfields.

Even with increased security, life in early gold-rush Melbourne was often challenging and sometimes dangerous. People struggled to find accommodation, and streets were crowded with diggers. Women sometimes felt unsafe, particularly after dark. Many men carried concealed firearms for safety. Diggers carried guns to protect their gold and possessions. Businessmen and storekeepers considered firearms essential for their protection.

Living in South Melbourne in 1853, William Kelly reported: 'I set out for a stroll in the neighbourhood, taking out as a bosom friend and companion a small revolver, as "sticking up" was quite common even in the mid-day in unfrequented places'. Fining a man heavily for firing a pistol in Little Bourke Street in 1852, a magistrate stated that he was: 'determined to put an end to the prevalent practice of firing guns or pistols in the city'.

27

The eastern end of Melbourne, 1858
Part of a panorama depicting Melbourne from Flagstaff Hill.
Lithographer – George Rowe. Source – State Library of Victoria

Mount Alexander Road, Flemington, about 1856
Winding its way north through Ascot Vale and Essendon,
Mt Alexander Road once formed the main route to the
Bendigo and Castlemaine goldfields. During the 1850s it
was trudged by tens of thousands of hopeful gold seekers
carrying awkward assortments of tools, parcels and bags.

Artist – Samuel Brees. Source – State Library of Victoria

The streets were dangerous in other ways. In the centre of town even the main city streets had open drains carrying sewage; animal carcasses rotted, or were eaten by stray dogs; and flies swarmed in summer. As Melbourne expanded, roads were hacked through the bush and soon became muddy bogs or dustbowls according to the season. The removal of trees gave the streets a barren appearance, and made walking in the height of summer without shade particularly unpleasant.

Other dangers threatened, too. Inadequate water and sewerage services saw devastating outbreaks of diseases such as typhoid, and infant mortality was high, particularly in the early years of the gold rush. Poorer people struggled to educate their children in the days before the introduction of free education.

But people adjusted to their circumstances, and many lived comfortable, safe lives, particularly on the elevated lands on the fringes of the city where larger homes were being built. Low-paid labourers and servants tilled the earth, grew vegetables and planted ornamental gardens, supporting the lives of the wealthy. Meanwhile, the majority lived frugally in small wooden and brick cottages.

The government did its part in establishing an orderly society. The Legislative Council drafted Victoria's constitution in 1853–54, introduced the world's first secret ballot and laid the foundations for responsible government in Victoria. On 23 November 1855 the *Constitution Act* was proclaimed, establishing two houses of parliament: the Legislative Assembly (the lower house) and the Legislative Council (the upper house). This structure has never been altered.

It was an optimistic start, but the government was slow to develop the desperately needed infrastructure. Public funds were limited, although some individuals held great personal wealth. With the abolition of the punitive gold licences in 1855, the government had only limited revenue, derived mainly from land sales and a gold export tax.

It adopted the British model of encouraging private investment in larger projects, such as railways, gasworks and even port facilities, while concentrating its own investment in water supply, postal and telegraph services and the colonial navy. Work on the city's water supply, gasworks and first railway finally began in 1853, heralded by grand gala events. All three projects would struggle to be completed amid escalating costs of materials and labour, technical problems and limited capital.

Canvas town, early 1850s

Artist – De Gruchy & Leigh. Source – State Library of Victoria

CANVAS TOWN

In the first months and years of the gold rush, thousands of arrivals in Melbourne had to be processed each week. Accommodation was difficult to find and a 'canvas town' sprang up on the south side of the Yarra, straddling St Kilda Road and covering a large area towards South Melbourne. Between 1852 and 1854, up to 7000 immigrants lived there at any one time.

Some tents were squalid and too small to stand in; others were large, and reinforced with timber slabs or iron. They were organised along streets, serviced by rough-shod stores, dining rooms and taverns. The streets became muddy in the rain, and in summer it was miserably hot. To make matters worse, fevers broke out. One man lost his wife and four children. Yet for all this, canvas town residents had to pay up to five shillings a week for a small site.

Broadsheet issued with the *Melbourne Morning Herald*, 11 November 1850

Just one year later, in 1854, the Melbourne & Hobsons Bay Railway Company opened Australia's first steam railway on the short route between the city and Sandridge (now Port Melbourne) on the shores of Hobsons Bay, where a deep-water pier served overseas sailing and steam ships. It was quickly followed by further privately funded railways to St Kilda (1857), Brighton (1859), Essendon (1860) and Hawthorn (1861).

Down by the West Melbourne swamp, Governor Charles Hotham lit the first fires in the gas company's retorts, but in the process he caught a chill and died before the supply of gas began a fortnight later, on New Year's Day 1856.

Newspaper editors lamented that the city streets, having first been dug up to lay gas pipes, were again disturbed so soon to lay water pipes. But it was worth the disruption: the first water from the Yan Yean Reservoir on the headwaters of the Plenty River reached the city in late 1857. A generation of grateful Melburnians would call a tap a 'Yan Yean'.

Institutions were also rapidly established in the first years of the gold rush. In the space of a few months in 1854, the National Museum of Victoria opened, the Public Library was founded, the first coach services ran to goldfields, the first telegraph line in Australia was set up between Melbourne and Williamstown, and the University of Melbourne and the *Age* newspaper were established.

The museum focused on natural history, economic botany and geology. Initially located at the Assay Office, in La Trobe Street, it was moved to the university in 1856 because of squabbling among interested parties and a cut to funding from government. But the museum quickly became popular. By 1860 annual visitor numbers passed 35 000, almost seven per cent of the colony's population. How many of these were the 'unskilled … gold seekers visiting the museum *en route* to the diggings' we cannot tell, but the museum's collection of models showing alluvial mining techniques underlined its role as an educational institution.

Education also underpinned the foundation of the Industrial and Technological Museum in 1870. The collection was formed from the National Museum of Victoria's mining and agricultural collections and material retained from the 1866 Intercolonial Exhibition. The National Museum of Victoria and the Industrial and Technological Museum would remain separate institutions until 1983, when they joined to form Museum Victoria.

TOKENS OF COMMERCE

In the first months and years following the discovery of gold, Melbourne grew so fast that there was insufficient coinage for people to shop with – particularly copper pennies and half pennies. Consequently, shopkeepers were allowed to issue copper tokens, as long as theirs looked different from the official currency.

Between 1849 and 1862, some 32 businesses in Melbourne had trade tokens bearing their names. The tokens pictured here were issued by Thrale & Cross (about 1854), Fenwick Brothers and Miller Brothers (1862).

The tokens provided a useful means of advertising businesses. Fenwick's store was located near Melbourne's flagstaff, one of the key landmarks of early Melbourne, and he used the flagstaff motif on his token to help customers find his store.

Collins Street, looking west across Elizabeth Street, 1854

Source – State Library of Victoria

Trade tokens

Fenwick Brothers and Miller Brothers tokens donated by George McArthur
Source – Museum Victoria

Queen Street between Lonsdale and Little Bourke Streets, about 1869

Photographer – John Noone. Source – State Library of Victoria

A home in the suburbs, about 1880

Photographer – J Linde Studio. Source – Museum Victoria

Other organisations were also paying attention to the natural landscape in mid-19th-century Melbourne. Edward Wilson, a private collector, founded the Victorian Acclimatisation Society in 1861. His motto was: 'if it lives, we want it'. The society introduced plants and animals to make the 'alien' Australian environment feel more like home, to beautify gardens, to provide sport for hunters and to 'aggrandise' the colony. But above all, it wanted to make the land economically productive.

The society worked alongside the Herbarium to introduce many alien species from other parts of Australia and from elsewhere in the world. An area of 20 hectares of Royal Park was set aside to house or process animals before their release; this led to the founding of Melbourne Zoo. Although many of the plant and animal species introduced were productive, some were later considered noxious or pests. The Acclimatisation Society folded about 1872, and the Zoological Society assumed the mantle of animal husbandry.

As Melbourne became more 'civilised' and economically powerful, there were increasing concerns that the city would be invaded by another alien force – a foreign navy sailing into Port Phillip Bay. The colonial ambitions of France, Germany and Russia in the Pacific were particularly feared. Local citizens established

volunteer army corps in the 1850s, which took over responsibility for the defence of the colony with the departure of the British army in 1870.

To repel enemy ships, fortifications and gun batteries were erected at the mouth of Port Phillip Bay, St Kilda, Brighton and Williamstown. In 1871, the Victorian Navy was strengthened with the purchase of HMVS *Cerberus*, a huge ironclad battleship. Its remnants now form a breakwater at Black Rock.

By the end of the 1870s, Melbourne had been transformed from a rough frontier port town into Australia's leading metropolis. Its citizens were favourably comparing their public facilities and infrastructure with those of leading cities in Britain and Europe. The latest technological advances quickly found advocates in Melbourne.

The gold rush changed Melbourne's entire economic structure too. The middle classes and artisans challenged the early pastoralists and merchants as leaders of Melbourne society, and the population mix changed. The Chinese community became the largest in Victoria after the British and Irish communities. Although Melbourne remained less culturally diverse than Victoria as a whole, its social fabric was changing.

Melbourne now stood at the brink of a remarkable economic boom, which would begin to create the city that we know today.

A LITTLE GREY FALCON

This Grey Falcon (*Falco hypoleucos*) flew into Surveyor-General Andrew Clarke's kitchen, near Merri Creek, in 1857 and tried to make off with a chicken. Clarke shot the falcon and donated it to the National Museum of Victoria (now Museum Victoria).

The museum had opened just three years earlier, initially building collections in natural history, economic botany and geology. These collections would provide a valuable record of Melbourne's natural history and bring Melburnians a greater knowledge of their newly adopted homeland.

Displays at the National Museum, *Illustrated Melbourne Post*, 1862

Artist – Samuel Calvert. Source – State Library of Victoria

Grey Falcon (*Falco hypoleucos*), 1857

Photographer – Rodney Start. Source – Museum Victoria

This quilt was made by Martha Bergin (later Tipping) in Queens County, Ireland, in 1843, when she was about 21 years old. It is a rare surviving example of a treasured possession brought to Melbourne during the gold rush.

The story of Martha and her husband, Andrew Tipping, is one of extraordinary loss and endurance. Six of their seven children died before adulthood – two in Ireland before they migrated in 1851.

The Tippings arrived in Melbourne at the height of the gold rush. Martha Tipping gave birth to James in Collins Street in 1852 – their only child to survive to adulthood. After losing another child they left Melbourne for the goldfields, moving from town to town seeking a living.

Why did so many of their children die? Poor sanitation and little knowledge of how disease occurred and could be treated caused high levels of mortality for both children and adults in the mid-19th century. One in five infants in Melbourne died in the 1850s.

THE FABRIC OF HOME

Martha Tipping (née Bergin), 1822–1883

Detail of Martha Bergin's quilt

Martha's father was a draper, which may explain the rich range of textiles incorporated in the quilt and its strong base fabric.

Donated by Dr Edmund Muirhead
Photographer – Rodney Start. Source – Museum Victoria

COBB & CO COACH

The road to the goldfields was a long one for people who had to walk. Few could afford a pack-horse or space on a dray.

Four young Americans, including Freeman Cobb, started Cobb & Co in 1853 to provide passenger transport between Melbourne and the goldfields. Their imported American 'thoroughbrace' coaches proved ideal for the rough bush roads. They developed a network of staging-posts, and employed drivers who knew the routes and stayed sober, ensuring a reliable and punctual service.

After the original partners sold out in 1855, others continued the name, and expanded services west and north across Victoria and beyond, always one step ahead of the growing railway network.

The coach pictured here is one of the few surviving original Cobb & Co coaches. It is believed to have been built in Geelong around 1880, and was designed to carry up to 17 passengers. Four or five horses would have pulled it. The coach was last used commercially in 1916 on the Casterton–Mount Gambier route.

Cobb & Co. coach, 1925

The coach was used for public relations purposes after it was retired from service.

Source – State Library of Victoria

Cobb & Co coach

Harley Dickson, a Geelong schoolboy, acquired the dilapidated coach in 1955. He restored it over many years and his family later donated it to the National Trust. Museum Victoria became its custodian in 2006 and undertook extensive conservation work.

Photographer – Jon Augier. Source – Museum Victoria

THE INFORMATION AGE BEGINS

The first electric telegraph line in Australia was set up in 1854, between Melbourne and Williamstown. The network used electrical signals to transfer information using a system known as Morse code. It expanded rapidly, and within five years it included lines to Geelong, Queenscliff and Ballarat, and a cable to Tasmania. By 1872, Australia was linked to Europe.

The telegraph became essential for government, commerce, railway, navigation, meteorology, astronomy and for news distribution. The telegraph was also used for entertainment. The first transmission of a horse race took place from Flemington Racecourse in 1859. In 1868, the Melbourne Chess Club defeated its Adelaide counterpart in a match played by telegraph.

This early demonstration Morse telegraph set, made at about half-scale, consists of a key, a sounder and a spring-driven inking register. It was displayed at the 1880–81 Melbourne International Exhibition.

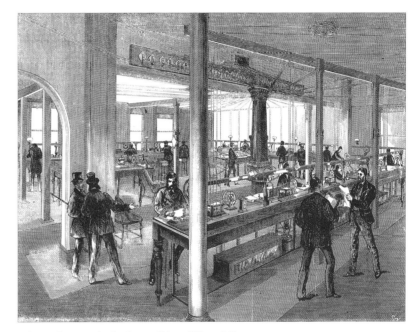

Telegraph centre in the General Post Office at the corner of Elizabeth and Bourke Streets, 1872

Source – State Library of Victoria

Morse telegraph model, 1880

Photographer – Jon Augier. Source – Museum Victoria

MARVELLOUS MELBOURNE   1880–1900

It wasn't just another parade. It was opening day of the 1880 Melbourne International Exhibition, the proudest moment of a booming city, spotlit on the world stage.

Eager crowds lined the route to the new Exhibition Building to watch parades of soldiers, sailors, firefighters and trade unionists. They were followed by a glittering convoy of state coaches. A burst of gunfire announced that the vice-regal party was on its way.

The exhibition would herald a decade of marvellous growth and optimism for Melbourne.

KEY DATES

1880 MELBOURNE'S POPULATION: **281 000**

1880 BUSHRANGER NED KELLY IS HANGED AT THE MELBOURNE GAOL

1880 MELBOURNE INTERNATIONAL EXHIBITION OPENS AT THE EXHIBITION BUILDING

1884 'OCTOPUS ACT' AUTHORISES AMBITIOUS SUBURBAN RAILWAY EXPANSION

1885 FIRST CABLE TRAM ROUTE OPENS

1887 LAND IN NEW SUBURBS SELLS FOR UP TO 20 TIMES MORE THAN THREE YEARS EARLIER

1888 ROYAL COMMISSION INVESTIGATES MELBOURNE'S POOR SANITATION

1888 MELBOURNE CENTENNIAL EXHIBITION OPENS AT THE EXHIBITION BUILDING

1888 NEW PRINCES BRIDGE IS COMPLETED OVER THE YARRA RIVER

1890 AUSTRALASIAN FEDERATION CONFERENCE IS HELD IN MELBOURNE, A STEP TOWARDS A UNITED AUSTRALIA

1891 IMPERIAL BANK SUSPENDS PAYMENTS, MARKING THE START OF VICTORIA'S WORST ECONOMIC DEPRESSION

1894 KALGOORLIE GOLD RUSH ATTRACTS THOUSANDS OF UNEMPLOYED MELBURNIANS TO WESTERN AUSTRALIA

1899 VICTORIAN TROOPS PARADE BEFORE EMBARKING FOR THE TRANSVAAL (BOER) WAR

1900 MELBOURNE'S POPULATION: **494 900**

In 1880, Melbourne was still basking in the prosperity and confidence generated by the world's richest gold rush. Then an extraordinary economic boom began, fuelled by frenzied speculation in land and company shares. The 1880–81 Melbourne International Exhibition and the 1888–89 Melbourne Centennial International Exhibition boasted Melbourne's achievements, and stimulated even more economic growth. Millions of visitors flocked to the exhibitions to see the latest industrial and artistic achievements from Australia, the British Empire and beyond, and to measure Victoria's progress against that of the rest of the world.

The signs of growth were everywhere. Swathes of new suburbs were appearing on Melbourne's fringes as if by magic: from Camberwell to Essendon, Footscray to Mentone. Suburban lifestyles, promoted by developers and estate agents, were embraced by middle-class and working-class buyers alike. Mansions sprang up around Melbourne's leafy perimeter as fortunes were made.

In central Melbourne, sumptuous new mercantile buildings changed the streetscape, many of them housing the 'land banks' and

building societies that were driving the boom. Lavishly decorated facades and intricate cast-ironwork trumpeted the wealth and achievements of the boom.

Evidence of the 1880s' land boom can still be seen in Melbourne. Opulent boom-style banking chambers and facades grace Collins Street. The years '1888' and '1889' are inscribed on thousands of buildings, from grand hotels to workers' cottages, and magnificent town halls in many municipalities.

Building 'Marvellous Melbourne' required vast quantities of materials and the labour of thousands of workers. Even using the latest machinery, Melbourne's brickworks, foundries and timber yards struggled to satisfy the demand for building supplies.

Other changes were also needed in the growing city. Infrastructure was massively expanded. Roads and footpaths now were paved, electric lighting began replacing gas street lamps and telephones rang in Collins Street. Suburban railway lines fanned out further and further from the city, and cable trams began to glide along the streets. A high-pressure water supply powered the lifts that made taller buildings possible. In private homes, gas cooking made life more comfortable and increasing numbers of houses were connected to running water.

The Melbourne International Exhibition
Colour supplement to the *Illustrated Australian News*, 1880
Lithographer – Sands & McDougall. Source – State Library of Victoria

A land sale by public auction on the outskirts of Melbourne

Developers offered free transport and refreshments to draw a crowd, creating a popular weekend pastime at the height of the boom.

Source – Public Record Office Victoria

Excavating Coode Canal at Fishermans Bend to straighten the lower Yarra River, 1883

Source – State Library of Victoria

Panorama of Melbourne, *Illustrated Australian News*, 1880

Engraver – Samuel Calvert. Source – State Library of Victoria

Melbourne in the boom-time may have been rich, but it still wasn't healthy. The city was choking on industrial and household filth. Slaughterhouses and other noxious trades soured the inner city and there was no sewerage system. Public health concerns led to the formation of the Melbourne and Metropolitan Board of Works, to build a sewerage system and increase the supply of clean water.

The Yarra River also needed attention. It had first been dredged for shipping in the 1840s, and later the Melbourne Harbour Trust widened the river below Princes Bridge, creating Coode Canal and cutting off Fishermans Bend. But floods still regularly swept down the Yarra, inundating the low-lying areas of Richmond and South Melbourne. The 1896 *Yarra Improvement Act* led to the river's realignment and beautification upstream from Princes Bridge.

Swept along by the confidence of the times, thousands of Melburnians invested in schemes to develop real estate and establish railways. Land banks and mortgage companies attracted money from small investors, then loaned it several times over to the builders and speculators. Money flowed in from Britain, fuelling the boom. By 1889, land values in parts of Melbourne were as high as those in central London. The city couldn't believe its luck.

Then came the inevitable crash. By 1893, most of the boom-time banks and land companies had collapsed, leaving their investors and depositors with nothing. Melbourne descended into its worst-ever economic depression. Investors, both large and small, faced ruin, and the entire community suffered. The worst effects of the depression lasted for the rest of the decade, but it would take the city many more years to recover.

The depression tore families apart. Perhaps one-third of Melbourne's workers were unemployed. Unable to pay the rent, many were evicted from their homes. Men went up-country or left for other colonies to seek work, leaving their families behind. Children were often victims of these desperate times. Some shared the experience of Clarice, an inmate of a children's refuge in La Trobe Street in 1897, who lamented: 'Me father couldn't keep me, an' me auntie couldn't keep me, an' me grandmother couldn't keep me…' (*Argus*, 1897).

Thousands of unemployed workers marched through the city and stormed the steps of Parliament House, demanding government work programs. Radical leader Chummy Fleming urged the homeless to demand accommodation in the Exhibition Building – but the building's doors stayed firmly shut.

43

MAKING A BETTER WORLD

Bessie Harrison Lee, 1860–1950

While many dreamt of a better world, Bessie Harrison Lee worked to make it happen.

After suffering abuse by drunken relatives as a child, Bessie Harrison Lee was raised by Christian guardians who stressed the importance of morality and self-control. A lack of education did not hamper her influence. She became a founder of the Women's Christian Temperance Union of Australia in 1891, campaigning for abstinence from alcohol as a solution to social problems. She also supported the campaign for women's right to vote.

At a time when men usually spoke on women's behalf, Bessie Harrison Lee was a rarity: a woman who lectured for a living. She gained an international following and campaigned into her 80s.

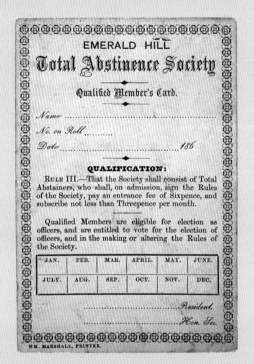

Membership card for the Emerald Hill Total Abstinence Society, about 1860–1870

Donated by the International Order of Good Templars
Source – Museum Victoria

Bessie Harrison Lee wearing her Women's Christian Temperance Union badge, about 1895

Photographer – Yeoman & Co. Source – National Library of New Zealand

Abstinence Society medals, about 1885

Medal on right donated by George McArthur
Source – Museum Victoria

Tess and Poll Hayes with a young relative, Cumberland Place, near Little Lon, 1901

Source – Museum Victoria

For other Melburnians, poverty had been part of their lives for far longer. In areas such as 'Little Lon' – the streets and lanes bordering Little Lonsdale Street near the central city – people crowded into tiny cottages abutting brothels, hotels and opium dens, and struggled every day to put food on the table. Prostitutes, families with children, drunks, nuns and tradesmen, all could be found living in Little Lon. The area was much feared, much imagined and much visited.

In spite of its reputation, Little Lon was home to new settlers from all parts of the world. Germans, Jews and Irish came in the mid-19th century; Chinese, southern Europeans and Syrians (Lebanese) in the 1880s; and Italians in the 1890s. By 1900, Little Lon was one of Australia's most multicultural neighbourhoods, although not as diverse as Melbourne's inner suburbs were to become after World War Two.

Life in Little Lon became even more challenging during the 1890s' depression. Stirred by the plight of Little Lon's residents, social reformers stepped in. Some worried that poverty caused immorality, whereas others thought: 'Drink … and love of idleness and excitement, appear to be among the principal causes of vice and crime' (Sister Esther of the Mission to the Streets and Lanes). Reformers were united in their concern for the young. Some set up schools and clubs in Little Lon. Others believed the solution lay in

'rescue work', removing young people from the inner city and providing homes and training in the garden suburbs.

Religious organisations were at the forefront of those trying to help. Wesley Mission, established in 1893 in Lonsdale Street, became a vocal advocate for social reform. It spoke against the sweatshops where impoverished men, women and children laboured, it lectured on the evils of drink and it offered a combination of worship, relief and institutional care. The Salvation Army established a women's shelter in Little Lon and held dramatic shows such as *Soldiers of the Cross*, using magic lanterns to project huge images onto public buildings in the city to convince people of the value of religion and morality. The Anglican Mission to the Streets and Lanes sought to 'Bring the message of the Gospel to the poor and fallen' (pamphlet promoting the Mission to the Streets and Lanes, 1885).

Beyond Little Lon, other Melbourne residents worked to create safer communities. In the absence of government support, benevolent Melburnians founded orphanages, aid societies, refuges, hospitals and other charitable institutions.

ABORIGINAL ACTIVISM

William Barak, 1824–1903

Aboriginal people have fought for their land and their rights since the time of European arrival. Residents of Coranderrk Aboriginal Station sent deputations to the Victorian government during the 1870s and 1880s, protesting their lack of rights and the threatened closure of their settlement.

The protestors were led by William Barak. Barak belonged to the Wurundjeri willam clan of the Woi wurrung. He was about 11 when Europeans began settling on his land. Barak was briefly educated at a mission school, where he learned to read, and later served in the Native Police.

Regardless of the protests, Coranderrk was scaled back. It continued as an Aboriginal reserve until 1924, when the remaining community was relocated to Lake Tyers in Gippsland. Healesville Sanctuary now occupies part of the original Coranderrk reserve.

Petition by Aborigines of Coranderrk to the Chief Secretary, 21 September 1886

On loan from Public Record Office Victoria

A group of Aboriginal men at Coranderrk, Healesville, late 19th century

Source – State Library of Victoria

Among the workless – feeding the hungry, Illustrated Australian News, **1890**

Source – National Library of Australia

Religious leaders preached against the greed and recklessness that was leading Victoria to the brink of ruin. Messages of temperance and healthy living from leaders such as Bessie Harrison Lee, founder of the Women's Christian Temperance Union of Australia, found a willing audience. Their social clubs, entertainment and public rallies offered a wholesome alternative to boozing, which could lead to drunkenness and family violence. Anti-liquor reformers built extravagant coffee palaces as alternatives to hotels and lobbied to restrict licensing laws.

Melbourne's tradition of social reform and justice saw significant achievements. In 1856, Melbourne workers were among the first in the world to win an eight-hour working day. From the mid-19th century workers began to form friendly societies to provide support in the event of accident or illness. Campaigns were held to unlock land held by squatters, resulting in land reform acts. And after 1872, all children were given free, compulsory, secular education.

Not all struggles were successful. Protests by residents of Coranderrk Aboriginal Station at their lack of rights and the threatened closure of their settlement fell on deaf ears. Neighbouring farmers wanted the fertile land, and from 1886 the government sought to integrate 'half-castes' into white society.

In the later years of the 19th century, a very different movement was also afoot: the push for Federation. Melbourne played a crucial role. It hosted the Australasian Federation Conference, which gave impetus to the campaign for a united Australia. Melbourne's leaders were soon preparing for a momentous event in the city's history: the opening of Australia's first parliament and the establishment of the nation's first seat of government. It would all happen in Melbourne

FROM BOOM TO BUST

James Munro, 1832–1908

A printer by trade and a devout Presbyterian, James Munro started a building society in 1865 to help workers each save for a home.

Munro became leader of the temperance movement in Melbourne, promoting sobriety and opposing the liquor trade. He helped establish grand coffee palaces, offering an alternative to the temptations of alcohol.

By the 1880s, Munro was a parliamentarian and wealthy businessman with diverse financial and manufacturing interests. To fuel his investments, he borrowed from his own companies.

Munro became premier of Victoria in 1890, just as the land boom was about to burst. Soon his own companies were in liquidation and Munro fled to London. He finished his days as a real estate agent in Armadale, Melbourne.

The Hon. James Munro, 1892

Source - City of Stonnington

The Grand Hotel, 1888

The 360-room Grand Hotel on Spring Street was Melbourne's largest luxury hotel when it was built in 1883. James Munro converted it to an alcohol-free 'coffee palace' in 1886 to promote temperance in Melbourne. It is now the Windsor Hotel.

Artist – A C Cooke. Engraver – E J McKaige. Source – Museum Victoria

A STREET BALLAD

'Marvellous Melbourne – The Latest Song on the Depression' is a rare surviving example of the street ballads sold on Melbourne's streets in the late 19th and early 20th centuries. They dealt with contemporary political, social and sporting events – in this case the unemployment and suffering caused by the 1890s' depression.

In 1885, visiting journalist George Augustus Sala had dubbed the city 'Marvellous Melbourne'. The locals embraced the title; but when Melbourne suffered its catastrophic economic collapse in the early 1890s, it became the focus for painful satire. This street ballad heightens the satire by setting the words to the American hit song of 1892, 'After the Ball'.

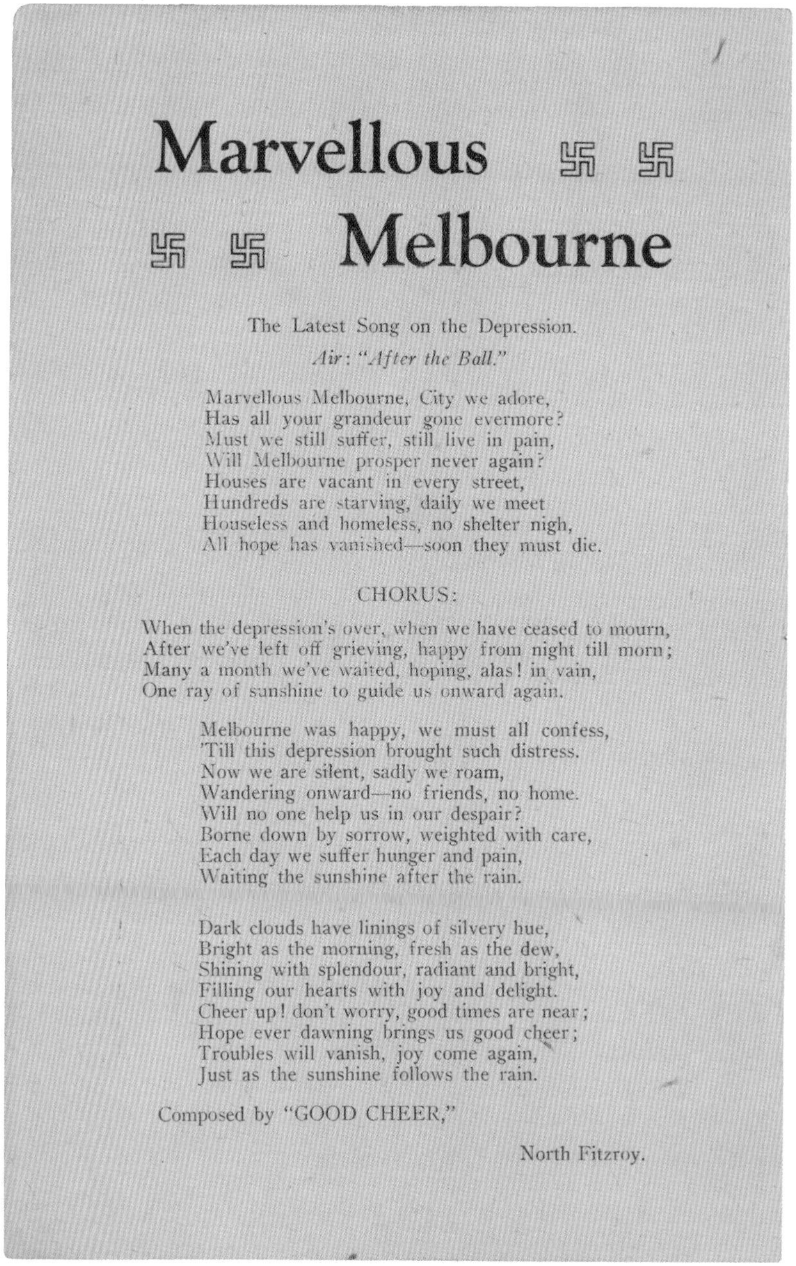

'Marvellous Melbourne – The Latest Song on the Depression', 1890s

The swastikas were probably included as decorations, and perhaps to denote good luck, without the ideological implications associated with their later use by the Nazis.

Source – Museum Victoria

Marvellous 卐 卐 卐 卐 Melbourne

The Latest Song on the Depression.

Air: "After the Ball."

Marvellous Melbourne, City we adore,
Has all your grandeur gone evermore?
Must we still suffer, still live in pain,
Will Melbourne prosper never again?
Houses are vacant in every street,
Hundreds are starving, daily we meet
Houseless and homeless, no shelter nigh,
All hope has vanished—soon they must die.

CHORUS:

When the depression's over, when we have ceased to mourn,
After we've left off grieving, happy from night till morn;
Many a month we've waited, hoping, alas! in vain,
One ray of sunshine to guide us onward again.

Melbourne was happy, we must all confess,
'Till this depression brought such distress.
Now we are silent, sadly we roam,
Wandering onward—no friends, no home.
Will no one help us in our despair?
Borne down by sorrow, weighted with care,
Each day we suffer hunger and pain,
Waiting the sunshine after the rain.

Dark clouds have linings of silvery hue,
Bright as the morning, fresh as the dew,
Shining with splendour, radiant and bright,
Filling our hearts with joy and delight.
Cheer up! don't worry, good times are near;
Hope ever dawning brings us good cheer;
Troubles will vanish, joy come again,
Just as the sunshine follows the rain.

Composed by "GOOD CHEER,"

North Fitzroy.

COLE'S BOOK ARCADE
Edward William Cole, 1832–1918

Edward William Cole and his book arcade exemplified the vigour and enterprise of Melbourne in the late 19th century. Cole emigrated from England in 1852, during the gold rush. Failing as a miner, he went into the retail business. In 1883 he opened a new, purpose-built store on the site of today's Bourke Street Mall.

Cole's Book Arcade was a shop like no other, crammed with new and second-hand books and other wares, but with the atmosphere of a circus. Cole enticed customers of all ages with a menagerie and fernery, a band, a clockwork symphonion and other mechanical delights.

Cole's 'Little Men' were manufactured in Melbourne for his arcade. They sat in the front window and passers-by could watch the Little Men turning the double crank handle. They were originally powered by running water.

Cole's Book Arcade closed in 1929, a decade after Edward William Cole's death.

One of the stores that made up Cole's Book Arcade

Sands & McDougall's Melbourne and Suburban Directory for 1890

Source – State Library of Victoria

COLE OF THE BOOK ARCADE. is as informative as it is entertaining.

Detail of 'Cole's Little Men'

Donated by A B Turnley. Photographer – Rodney Start.
Source – Museum Victoria

A SYMBOL OF SUCCESS

James Fergusson proudly moved into his grand new Malvern home, 'Glenferrie', in 1872. It was a two-storey mansion, with 14 rooms and extensive grounds. James Fergusson was a co-owner of one of the leading printing firms in the colony and had recently been elected to the Victorian Parliament.

This window was located in a large stairwell at 'Glenferrie'. The style of the window indicates that it was locally made by Ferguson & Urie, the main stained-glass manufacturers in Melbourne from the early 1860s to the 1890s.

The window celebrates James Fergusson's success and illustrates the colony's pride and continuing attachments to Britain. The Australian coat of arms appears at the top; the thistle, rose and shamrock (symbols of Scotland, England and Ireland) are repeated throughout the background. Pride of place is given to the Fergusson blazon of arms.

Stained-glass window

Donated by Richard and Catherine Price, through the Australian Government's Cultural Gifts Program

Photographer – Benjamin Healley. Source – Museum Victoria

Detail of the window showing a printing press

MELBOURNE AND THE NATION 1900–1920

It was the most magnificent crowd Melbourne had ever seen: 12 000 of Australia's leading lights, dressed in their finest frock coats, uniforms and gowns, glittering with jewels, rustling in starched cotton and velvet, breathing the same air as the Duke of Cornwall and York – the future King George V.

Seated beneath the soaring dome of the Exhibition Building, they were waiting for the glorious moment: the opening of Australia's first parliament, in Australia's first capital city – Melbourne.

KEY DATES

1900 Melbourne's population: **494 900**

1901 Sydney's population surpasses Melbourne's for the first time since 1861

1901 Melbourne becomes the temporary capital of the newly federated Australia

1901 'White Australia policy' and national import tariffs are introduced

1902 Women win the right to vote in federal elections; women not permitted to vote in Victorian elections until 1908

1906 Release of *The Story of the Kelly Gang*, the world's first feature-length film, made in Melbourne

1906 Suburban electric tram services are introduced in Melbourne

1907 Harvester Judgement in Melbourne establishes the 'basic wage' for Australian men

1910 New Flinders Street Station opens

1912 Luna Park opens

1914 World War One begins, ending in 1918

1918 Worldwide influenza pandemic strikes Melbourne

1920 Melbourne's population: **763 000**

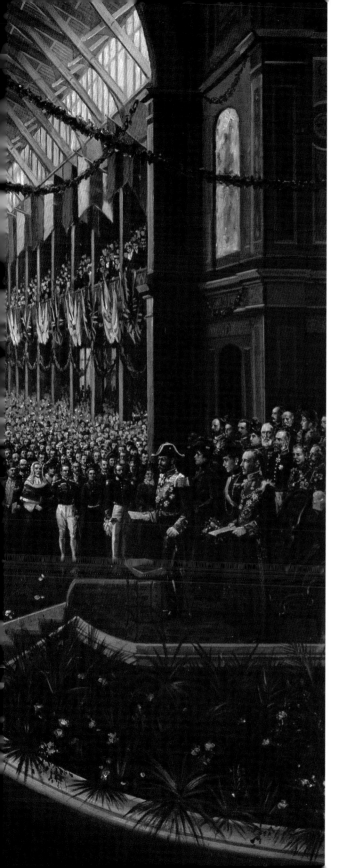

At the turn of the century Melbourne was swept by a wave of national pride. The city was the first capital of the newly federated Australia. Some '12 000 people seated in a vast amphitheatre – free people, hopeful people, courageous people – entrusted with working out their own destiny and rejoicing in their liberty' crammed Melbourne's Exhibition Building to witness the opening of Parliament (*Argus*, 10 May 1901).

Australians began to think of themselves as 'Australian' and to celebrate the achievements of their shared colonial past. But not everyone had cause to celebrate. The first act passed by the Australian government was the *Immigration Restriction Act 1901*, limiting the entry of non-European migrants. And Aboriginal Australians were denied basic rights, such as the right to vote in federal elections.

As national capital, Melbourne was at the centre of the movement for a 'white Australia'. Prominent among the organisations staunchly supporting trade protection and immigration restriction was the Australian Natives' Association – 'native' here meaning Australia-born. While the gold rush and its aftermath had brought people to the city from many countries,

the overwhelming majority of Melburnians were of British or Irish ancestry – and shared a hope that Australia would remain that way. In 1902, Prime Minister Edmund Barton declared:

We can bring in, without delay, our kinsmen from Britain and, if the numbers be insufficient, such other white races as will assimilate with our own. Or we can ... see the doors of our house forced, and streams of people from the lands where there is hardly standing room pour in and submerge us.

Closely linked to the idea of a 'white Australia' were questions about the sort of nation Australia should be and how it should be symbolised. Native fauna and flora – the kangaroo, emu and wattle – emerged as popular symbols of a new national identity and took their place on Australia's new coat of arms. Wattle Day, Arbor Day and Bird Day all emerged in the years following Federation. They celebrated 'true Australian aspirations, fulfilments and life' and a distinctive sense of nationhood.

From the 1880s, the Heidelberg School of artists (Australian Impressionists) had painted evocative images of the bush and farmlands around Melbourne, helping to develop the Australian identity. Their art fed into a movement to promote Australian nature as a civilising and moralising influence, and to redeem the bush from its 'hostile' image.

Print of *Opening of the first Commonwealth Parliament of Australia by H.R.H. the Prince of Wales*, 1902

Artist – Charles Nuttall. On loan from Healesville Historical Society

CELEBRATING THE NATION

The overwhelming importance of Federation drove a huge demand for souvenirs. Governments and other organisations commissioned medals featuring royalty, Lord Hopetoun (the first Governor-General of Australia), mottos, flags, state emblems and symbolic imagery. Invitations to Federation events were lavishly printed, rosettes were proudly pinned onto starched clothes, and menus were savoured and then carefully stored away. Portable cameras allowed the technically-minded to take snapshots as personal mementoes, and stereoscopic cards reminded people of how it felt to be there.

This invitation to a 'conversazione' in Melbourne's Exhibition Building is addressed to Inspecting Superintendent of Police Mr T O'Callaghan and Mrs O'Callaghan. A conversazione was an evening event, usually of intellectual nature, with discussions about literature, art or science.

Hosted by the government of Victoria, the conversazione was part of a glittering program of events in May 1901 to celebrate Federation. While official guests enjoyed the receptions, concerts and dinners, out on the streets fireworks lit the night sky, bands played and processions rumbled along streets decorated with ceremonial arches, painted banners and fluttering flags.

Invitation, 'Conversazione in the Exhibition Building', 1901

G B H Austin, an architect in the Victorian Public Works Department, designed the invitation. The lithograph was made at Sands & McDougall.

On loan from Arts Victoria – gift from Arthur and Caroline Howard Bequest

Medal, Australian Commonwealth, 1901

Source – Museum Victoria

Cootamundra Wattle (*Acacia baileyana*), 1921
Archibald James Campbell was a passionate advocate for
the protection of Melbourne's native flora and fauna. A field
naturalist and collector of birds and eggs, he was also a
photographer and prolific writer.

Campbell helped inaugurate the first national Wattle Day,
held on 1 September 1910. Wattle Day became an important
celebration of national identity and the natural environment.

This photograph features his daughter Elizabeth.

Photographer – A J Campbell
Published in *Golden Wattle – Our National Floral Emblem*, 1921

At the same time, early environmentalists called
for the protection of native vegetation and
wildlife from the impacts of suburban expansion
around Melbourne. They drew on the prevailing
mood of national pride to argue their cause, and
linked the welfare of nature to the moral welfare
of the community.

It was a time of change for Melbourne. As well
as standing centre-stage in the development
of the Australian identity as the first national
capital, Melbourne witnessed many of the new
ideas about government and society that were
circulating globally. Some were radical and
many impractical; others would change society
forever.

Ideals of social democracy ran deep in Victoria,
having already led to such advances as free
education and greater equality for all classes
of men. Gender inequality was slower to be
addressed, but progress was finally underway.
From 1908, women in Victoria were allowed
to vote – the last Australian state to grant that
right.

Some of the new ideas focused on defining
limits to rights and opportunities. Fearing that
women, immigrants and minorities would take
jobs, trade unions urged restrictions on labour.
The eugenics movement promoted the 'science'
of racial purity, in parallel to the push for a white
Australia.

Capitalism was reinvented as 'welfare
capitalism'. By supporting the lives of workers
with housing, health care and entertainment,
businessmen hoped to ensure a stable,
dependent workforce and to curtail trade
unionism. Hugh Victor McKay established the
suburb of Sunshine to house the workforce for
his Sunshine Harvester Works, which made
agricultural and other machinery. He located the
business just beyond the existing jurisdiction of
the Wages Board. The business prospered, but
McKay's wage strategy came unstuck when
the workers fought and won a case for better
wages. The landmark Harvester Judgement
set a minimum wage for unskilled labourers
throughout Australia.

More altruistic concerns prompted action on
the living conditions for many in Melbourne,
especially in the crowded inner suburbs. Large
cities were likened to cancers, spreading
disease and sapping the nation's strength. The
state government's Closer Settlement Scheme
was established in 1904 to entice people away
from the inner city. Smallholdings for farming
were made available throughout the state. In
Melbourne, land was subdivided for workers'
homes in the fringe suburbs of Footscray,
Brunswick, Northcote and Thornbury, and for
'clerks' in the eastern suburbs of Glenhuntly and
Tooronga.

THE CHEN FAMILY

The 1901 *Immigration Restriction Act* was one of several new laws restricting migrant entry to Australia and curtailing the rights of existing non-European residents. For example, after 1903, Australian-born Chinese men were denied the right to bring their wives and children into Australia.

Chen Ah Kew had arrived during the gold rush, and later brought his Chinese wife to Victoria. They moved back to China with their six children in 1901. As adults, the sons returned to Melbourne, forming Wing Young & Co., wholesale fruit merchants. Despite the sons' Australian origins, the new laws meant that their Chinese-born wives were denied permanent residence here. The women were forced to live a precarious existence on temporary visas, accepted and denied entry at the discretion of government officials.

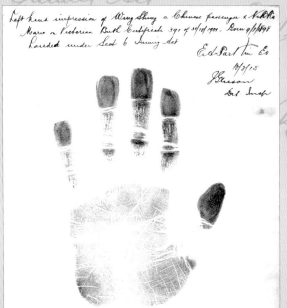

Handprint of Peter Wing Shing, 1915

This handprint was required as proof of identity in order for Peter Wing Shing to re-enter Australia, the country of his birth.

Source – National Archives of Australia

Three generations of the Chen family in Melbourne, 1928

Source – Wang family

Workers' houses on a Closer Settlement Scheme estate, about 1910

Source – Museum Victoria

By 1916, about 1000 homes had been built. Residents struggled for years, however, to get basic amenities such as roads, water supply and sewerage. The Closer Settlement Scheme was ultimately considered a failure, even though it was used as a model for soldier settlement schemes after World War One – also largely a failure.

Concerns for other Melburnians led to the construction of the city's largest building. It wasn't a hotel, market or Parliament House – it was an asylum. Kew Asylum was built in 1872 for 435 patients; by 1912 it housed three times that number. The prevailing approach to mental illness encouraged treatment in large institutions, but the great numbers of patients overwhelmed the staff. Patients with psychiatric or intellectual disabilities were crowded together with those suffering dementia or alcoholism. In large dormitories in echoing buildings, they followed a routine regulated by the asylum bell. Many worked – in the garden, preparing food, cleaning or washing clothes. Others were left idle. Mental illness was little understood and patients at Kew rarely saw a doctor. Although enforced rest and a regular routine helped many patients, others languished for decades behind the asylum walls.

While Melbourne tried to deal with its internal challenges, larger troubles were brewing far away in the northern hemisphere. With the outbreak of World War One, the young nation of Australia sent its army to fight distant battles in Europe and the Middle East.

Melburnians were quick to show their loyalty. Two out of every five men aged 18 to 44 enlisted voluntarily in the military, many in the 2nd Brigade, which took part in the Anzac landing at Gallipoli on 25 April 1915. Within a fortnight one-third were dead or wounded. A year later the reinforced brigade was fighting in the front-line trenches at Pozieres in France.

Women played a vital role, too. Some went to the front as nurses, while others raised funds to buy ambulances and guns, and organised food, clothing and newspapers for soldiers at the front through the Comforts Fund.

Melburnians were divided during the war by a bitter debate over compulsory military service. Irish Catholics were unwilling to support Britain at a time when Ireland was pressing for independence. Protestants were more inclined to support the war. The majority of Victorians voted in favour of conscription in 1916, but a year later, with casualty lists growing, many had changed their minds. (As a nation, Australians voted against conscription at both referenda.)

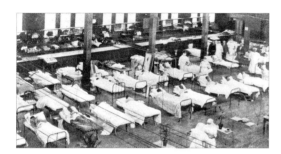

Men's ward in the Exhibition Building during the Spanish flu pandemic

Published in the *Sydney Mail*, 1919.
Source – Museum Victoria

By the end of the war, two-thirds of the forces had been killed or wounded, leaving scarcely a family untouched. Many men returned damaged, shell-shocked, bitter and broken. Even those whose men hadn't gone to war were suffering. Old certainties about civilisation and the value of human life were shaken. Yet the sacrifices made seemed to confirm Australia's status on the world stage, and a growing sense of national identity was reinforced by the creation of the 'Anzac legend'.

More heartache was to follow. As troops around the world returned to their home countries, they took with them the most devastating pandemic of modern times: the Spanish flu. It arrived in Melbourne in late 1918, and by early 1919 thousands had fallen ill. Many public places – cinemas, schools and racecourses – were closed and people wore masks to slow the spread of the virus. A temporary hospital was opened in the Exhibition Building, accommodating more than 4000 people. The flu claimed the lives of nearly 2500 Melburnians during those terrible months.

The Commonwealth Serum Laboratories (CSL) worked determinedly to develop an effective vaccine. Based in Melbourne, it had been established to produce biopharmaceuticals locally during World War One, when Australia was cut off from its usual sources of vaccines and other bacteriological products. It produced millions of doses of a mixed bacterial vaccine to fight the flu. But it was not then known that the flu was caused by a virus, not a bacterium, and the vaccine was ineffective. CSL went on to become a world leader in such areas as penicillin, insulin, antivenoms, vaccines and blood products.

Other scientific organisations based in Melbourne during and immediately after the war placed the city at the forefront of Australian scientific research, including the Council for Scientific and Industrial Research (later known as CSIRO), the agricultural Research Farm, the Walter and Eliza Hall Institute, the Bureau of Meteorology and the Defence Department's chemical laboratory.

The future looked promising for Melbourne, but the dark clouds of depression and war loomed again.

Bourke Street, Melbourne, early 1900s

Source – Alexander Turnbull Library, New Zealand

'NOT FIT TO BE AT HOME'

The story of William Douglas was a familiar one to many residents of Kew Asylum.

William Douglas was 31 when his family admitted him in 1908. Except for a few short periods, he would spend the rest of his life at Kew: he was thought 'not fit to be at home'.

Upon admission, William Douglas was assessed as 'confusional, depressed and despondent'. His behaviour was similar in 1909, 'unable to do anything', and 1911, 'no fixity of purpose'. He was pronounced incurably insane in 1912, and died four years later.

William Douglas's misfortune was that his family did not want him at home, despite his being in good health and even, for a time, 'improved mentally and physically'. As a single man without family support or steady employment, William Douglas was condemned to his fate.

William Douglas on admission to Kew Asylum, 1908

Source – Public Record Office Victoria

Kew Asylum, about 1890

Source – State Library of Victoria

Letter from Kew Asylum's male patient register

Written by Alexander Douglas to the medical superintendent, 30 August 1910, this letter is still pinned to the record of William Douglas, patient number 6558.

On loan from Public Record Office Victoria

Aug. 30/10
144 Curzon St
North Melbourne

The Medical Superintendant

Dear Sir

My Brother William Douglas wrote to you for his Discharge I thought it only right to let you know that he was in one of his bad Tempers when he wrote of cours I understand that You are the best judge whet wether he should have it I would esteem it a great favour if you would please not to mention to him that I have been asking for his Probation to be extended all along because if he knew that there will be no living with him

Yours Faithfully
Alexander Douglas

A SOLDIER'S STORY

Albert Kemp, 1884–1917

dear daddy I am waiting and watching day by day for you.

Young Ethel Kemp wrote these words to her father, Albert, who was away fighting in World War One. She would never see him again.

Albert Kemp was a Caulfield butcher with a wife, Annie, and two children, Ethel and George, when he enlisted in 1916. Just 21 days later he embarked for England, and after less than 12 weeks' training he was sent to the Western Front. Within six months Albert was dead.

His family's loss was made worse when his belongings were mistakenly sent to the family of another Albert Kemp, who had also died in the war. Annie Kemp struggled financially for years, and was eventually evicted from her home. She never re-married.

Postcard, 'Fond Thoughts of You'

Source – Museum Victoria

Private Albert Edward Kemp

Source – Museum Victoria

A MARVEL OF ENTERPRISE

Hugh Victor McKay, 1865–1926

H V McKay was born in 1865 and grew up on a farm near Elmore, Victoria. Frustrated by the slow, laborious nature of farm work, he searched for a more efficient way to harvest wheat.

At the age of 18, McKay developed a stripper harvester, a machine that revolutionised farming in Australia and overseas. By the 1920s, McKay's Sunshine Harvester Works was the largest manufacturing plant in Australia, with more than 1600 workers and 26 hectares under roof. McKay established an entire suburb to house his workers – the suburb of Sunshine.

A 'marvel of enterprise, energy and pluck', McKay was lauded for his vision and his remarkable achievements as a manufacturer and exporter. Yet his success has often been overshadowed by criticism of his opposition to trade unionism and wage regulation.

McKay used this model of his stripper harvester on his promotional tour of Russia in 1912. There has been much controversy over McKay's claim that he invented the stripper harvester. While McKay's stripper was the first on the market in 1886, Melburnian James Morrow had patented and exhibited a stripper harvester more than a year earlier. McKay claimed to have no knowledge of Morrow's work.

McKay stripper harvester 1899 model, 1:5 scale model
Donated by H V McKay Pty Ltd.
Photographer – Rodney Start. Source – Museum Victoria

Hugh Victor McKay, 1912
Source – Museum Victoria

MELBOURNE'S DIVA

Dame Nellie Melba, 1861–1931

If you wish to understand me at all, you must understand first and foremost that I am an Australian.

In September 1902, Nellie Melba (Helen Porter Mitchell) returned triumphant to her hometown of Melbourne, after 16 years in Europe. A public holiday was proclaimed to welcome the operatic diva, and the city was hectic with people, bands and flags. Following the pomp and pride of Federation, Melburnians now revelled in the glory of Melba's worldwide fame – and in the homage paid to their city by her stage name.

Her concerts at the Town Hall were sell-outs. As an encore, Melba sang what was to become her signature piece and local tribute, 'Home Sweet Home'.

Melba bought a home in the Yarra Valley in 1909 and spent many of the war years there raising money. Her numerous farewell concerts during the 1920s saw 'more farewells than Nellie Melba' enter the vernacular. But her final farewell, in 1931, saw people line the funeral route all the way from Scots Church in the city to Lilydale Cemetery.

Studio portrait of Nellie Melba, early 1900s

Publisher – J Beagles & Co., London. Source – National Library of Australia

Leather pouch, rosary beads and chatelaine

Worn by Melba as Marguerite in Gounod's opera *Faust* in 1924. The beads and chatelaine were probably also worn by Melba for the same role earlier in her career.

Photographer – Benjamin Healley
On loan from the Performing Arts Collection

ELECTRIC CITY   1920–1945

It was an overcast day in February 1921. Returned war hero General Sir John Monash, now in charge of the State Electricity Commission, stood in a windswept Gippsland paddock with his pipe in one hand and a roll of drawings in the other.

He had come to witness a start to the construction of Victoria's greatest industrial enterprise – the harnessing of brown coal to generate cheap and 'clean' electric power for Melbourne.

If there was a single moment when Melbourne entered the electric age, this was it.

KEY DATES

1920 MELBOURNE'S POPULATION: **763 000**

1924 MELBOURNE'S FIRST RADIO STATION STARTS TRANSMISSION

1927 FEDERAL PARLIAMENT MOVES FROM MELBOURNE TO THE NEW NATIONAL CAPITAL, CANBERRA

1929 START OF THE GREAT DEPRESSION

1930 PHAR LAP WINS THE MELBOURNE CUP

1932 AUSTRALIAN ABORIGINES' LEAGUE FORMED IN FOOTSCRAY TO FIGHT FOR ABORIGINAL RIGHTS

1934 MAJOR FLOOD OF THE YARRA RIVER

1934 SHRINE OF REMEMBRANCE IS OPENED

1935 CENTENARY OF MELBOURNE IS CELEBRATED

1938 HOUSING COMMISSION OF VICTORIA IS FORMED TO CREATE AFFORDABLE PUBLIC HOUSING

1939 'BLACK FRIDAY' BUSHFIRES ACROSS VICTORIA KILL 71 PEOPLE

1939 WORLD WAR TWO BEGINS, ENDING IN 1945

1940 LAST CABLE TRAM RUNS IN MELBOURNE

1945 MELBOURNE'S POPULATION: **1 180 200**

After World War One, the winds of change blew through Melbourne. New styles of houses began to appear in the growing suburbs: Californian bungalow, Spanish mission, Tudor revival and streamlined moderne. Inside the home, cluttered Victorian mantelpieces were stripped bare, heavy curtains were flung away and cabinets were built into modern kitchens.

Most new suburbanites enjoyed conveniences unimaginable just a few decades earlier: electric lights, gas stoves and heaters, flushing toilets and, for some, telephones – although many poor households waited until after World War Two to even get running water.

In the city centre, too, things were changing. Office buildings were growing ever larger and more daring, proud symbols of ambition and success. The sound of the city was becoming louder: telephones rang, electric trams rattled along the streets and motor cars spluttered. In offices and factories, workers were enjoying the safety and convenience of electricity. Technology had made it all possible.

Of all the changes in Melbourne between the wars, improvements to the electricity supply were arguably the most significant technologically. Melburnians were first dazzled by electric light in the 1880s, when a limited electrical supply by private operators lit the central city streets and began powering industry.

Early steam-powered generators relied on imported black coal, mainly from New South Wales. Strikes by miners and maritime workers frequently disrupted Victorian industry and eventually led to the formation of the government-owned State Electricity Commission of Victoria (SEC) in 1920. Headed by Sir John Monash, the SEC began to build Victoria's first brown-coal-fired power station, at Yallourn in the Latrobe Valley. It was a massive project requiring technical innovation and complex organisation. Electricity started flowing from Yallourn in 1924.

The impact on Melbourne life was dramatic. On the streets, electrification of Melbourne's public transport made tram and train travel more comfortable and efficient, and helped shape suburban expansion during the 1920s and 1930s. Electric trams were introduced from 1906, as extensions to the railways and cable tram routes. The formation of the Melbourne and Metropolitan Tramways Board in 1920 created a unified tram system.

View of Bourke Street, facing Parliament House, illuminated for Melbourne's centenary, 1934–35

Photographer – Roy Leibig. Source – Museum Victoria

Welcoming the first electric train to Thomastown, 16 December 1929

Poster advertising tram and train services to a new estate in Hawthorn, 1925

The board introduced a new standard electric tram design and began the task of converting aging cable tram routes.

Planning for train electrification started in 1907, and construction of Newport Power Station to generate electricity for the train network began in 1913. After delays caused by World War One, Melbourne's first electric train services began operation in May 1919 between Essendon and Sandringham. Within four years, all suburban lines were electrified.

In private homes, electricity spread more slowly. Before the 1920s, few Melbourne homes used electricity. Not only was the supply unreliable and prices high, but also many people feared electrocution. Most were satisfied with gas, kerosene, coal or firewood for their light, heating and cooking needs.

With Yallourn power station completed in 1924, the SEC set to work promoting the use of electricity in the home. Its campaign was a success. Melbourne's electricity consumption increased eightfold between 1920 and 1940, and by 1950 nearly all Melbourne homes were wired for electricity. Even so, many Melburnians limited their electricity use to lighting and a few small appliances, such as irons. Only in the 1950s did 'white goods' – electric fridges, washing machines and stoves – become standard household items.

As electricity spread into huge new suburban housing estates in the 1920s, Melbourne was experiencing its greatest building boom since the 1880s. And like the 1880s, a devastating bust followed. This time, though, the bust was not the result of a collapse in local speculation, but rather a slowing economy, falling exports, rising unemployment and the withdrawal of British investment. The bust was precipitated by a world economic crisis, which began with the collapse of the New York stock exchange in December 1929. The effects rapidly reverberated around the world.

Melbourne was hit hard by the Great Depression. Wealthy shareholders lost fortunes overnight. Jobs disappeared, especially in the poorer manufacturing suburbs. The homeless and jobless queued for food and charity 'handouts' in an age before unemployment benefits. By 1933, almost one-third of unemployed men had been out of work for three years.

In response, the state government set up public works projects and provided basic sustenance ('susso') for workers. The workers, known as 'sussos', created suburban parks, the Shrine of Remembrance, the Yarra Boulevard and even the Great Ocean Road. Governments also acknowledged that full employment was a central policy objective for the first time.

THE BIG DIPPER RIDES AGAIN

The Big Dipper was Luna Park's most popular thrill ride from its arrival in 1923 until it closed in 1988. It offered more speed with steeper climbs and descents than the old Scenic Railway. There were originally three sets of trains in use, each of which had three carriages joined together.

Museum Victoria acquired this Big Dipper carriage several years after the ride was closed. The museum undertook extensive restoration of the carriage in 2007, including replacing rotted timbers and reupholstering the seats. Paint-layer analysis was undertaken, and the carriage was returned to its original colour scheme. Visitors are once again welcome to sit in the carriage.

Crowds at Luna Park, 1942

Photographer – Roy Leibig. Source – Museum Victoria

The restored Big Dipper carriage

Photographer – Benjamin Healley. Source – Museum Victoria

Better times were ahead for most Melburnians, as social services improved and the economy began to strengthen. During the 1930s the manufacturing sector gradually recovered, and the outbreak of World War Two provided the economic stimulus to finally dispel the last effects of the Great Depression.

Melburnians also found many ways to keep their spirits up. In the pre-television age, people flocked in their thousands to Melbourne's grand picture palaces for the latest talking pictures. Newsreels kept Melburnians in touch with current events – the triumphs of Phar Lap, breadlines during the Depression, Melbourne's centenary celebrations and Australia's involvement in World War Two.

An evening at the cinema was a big night out. One ticket entitled its holder to two features, several newsreels and a cartoon. Although the cinemas were grand in style, tickets were affordable to ordinary wage earners. Several landmark Melbourne cinemas, including the still-surviving Capitol (1924) in Swanston Street and the Regent (1929) in Collins Street, were built to accommodate the growing audiences.

Although the Depression decimated ticket sales, Melbourne's cinemas were thriving again by the end of World War Two, helped by the wartime influx of American servicemen.

Another place for Melburnians to play was Luna Park. It had opened by the bay in St Kilda in 1912, and owed much to the brash new amusement parks that had sprung up along the beaches of North America. Gaudily decorated with thousands of electric lights, even its name came from a famous seaside funfair in New York.

Melburnians quickly made Luna Park their own, with more than 22 000 people attending the opening celebrations. Soon up to 10 000 patrons were visiting each Saturday night, taking to heart Luna Park's motto 'Just for fun'. Crowds flocked through the iconic 'smiling moon' face, eager to ride the park's main drawcards – the Scenic Railway, which still encircles the park, and the supreme thrill machine, the Big Dipper, which was added in 1923.

Of course, there were other ways to have fun in Melbourne and some are still familiar: picnics in the gardens, backyard cricket or a good book from the local library. As car ownership increased, more families headed to the Dandenongs or the beach for a day out, or loaded up the car for a camping trip. Australian Rules football fans crowded onto trains and trams, crossing the city to support their local heroes every Saturday afternoon from April to September. Horseracing became the focus of the public imagination when the champion racehorse Phar Lap won the 1930 Melbourne Cup, then died dramatically in 1932 in California at the height of his career.

During 1934–35, there was another major focus for Melburnians: celebrations to herald the 100th anniversary of the European settlement of Victoria and Melbourne. Nostalgia shaped the events, with a parade between Port Melbourne and the Melbourne Town Hall marking the launch of celebrations by the Duke of Gloucester. Melburnians were glad of the chance to dress in pioneer costume and focus on the achievements of their city's founders. An 18th-century cottage belonging to the parents of explorer and navigator Captain James Cook was brought stone by stone from Yorkshire and re-erected in the Fitzroy Gardens – although Cook's connection to Melbourne was questionable. An air race between London and Melbourne, funded by confectionery entrepreneur and philanthropist Macpherson Robertson, attracted international attention to the city.

Pioneer John Batman was elevated to hero status and featured in much of the centennial iconography. The 'pristine wilderness' of the Yarra River *then* was contrasted with the modern city skyline *now*. That theme was reflected in a commemorative stamp in which an Aboriginal man surveys modern Melbourne from the banks of the Yarra.

A MAN OF ENERGY

Sir John Monash, 1865–1931

When Sir John Monash was appointed to head the State Electricity Commission in June 1920, he was already regarded as the greatest living Australian.

An engineer by profession, Monash pioneered reinforced concrete construction in Australia. But it was his commanding role in World War One, leading Australian and Allied troops to victory on the Western Front, that made him a national hero.

A leader of Monash's calibre was just the person to steer the SEC through its turbulent first decade. In the face of awesome technical challenges, political opposition and strident media criticism, he helped create one of Australia's most successful public enterprises.

In his last years, Monash was chief organiser of Melbourne's Anzac Day march and he oversaw construction of the Shrine of Remembrance. When he died in 1931, an estimated 250 000 mourners lined the streets of Melbourne for his state funeral.

Sir John Monash, about 1931

Photographer – Lafayette-Sarony, Melbourne. Source – National Library of Australia

A clandestine acquisition

In May 1919, General Monash was asked by the Victorian agent general to help 'liberate' technical secrets from German brown-coal-mining companies in the Rhine Valley. Monash immediately dispatched one of his most trusted deputies, Major Noel Mulligan.

In just four weeks of clandestine activity, Mulligan amassed a large collection of engineering drawings, photographs and technical data, including this working model of the latest German briquette press design. The information was to prove enormously valuable to the SEC in its development of Victoria's brown-coal resources.

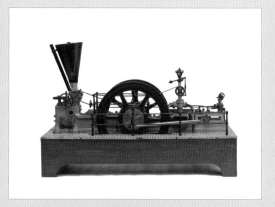

Briquette press model, about 1919

Donated by the State Electricity Commission of Victoria
Photographer – Rodney Start. Source – Museum Victoria

Trench digging at Fawkner Park, South Yarra, about 1942

Source – State Library of Victoria

Four years after Melbourne celebrated its centenary, World War Two broke out. Thousands of Melburnians enlisted to fight or joined the war effort at home. Units raised in Melbourne included the 2/5th and 2/6th Battalions of the 6th Division, which saw action in Libya, Syria, Greece and New Guinea. The war at first seemed remote to many Melburnians, but when Japan entered the conflict in December 1941, Allied armed forces were increasingly visible on Melbourne's streets and the fear of bombing hung in the air. The city was considered vulnerable to enemy attack, as its industrial and port facilities were centralised, so anti-aircraft guns were installed at key locations such as Maribyrnong and Middle Park.

The community swung into action, with 60 000 volunteering for air-raid precaution duties. Women volunteered for the Australian Comforts Fund and the Red Cross, and even Boy Scouts were asked to deliver telephone messages by bicycle if the telephone lines were cut. Women joined the workforce in place of the men who had gone to fight, and by 1944 one-quarter of those in the workforce were women.

Many worked in the booming manufacturing sector, as aircraft and munitions factories increased their outputs for the war effort.

The war was a turning point for Melbourne, socially, culturally and economically. The city stood at the brink of its largest social change ever: the arrival of postwar immigrants and an economic boom.

A TRUE LEGEND

Melbourne's most famous horse was born in New Zealand. Trained in Australia, he became a local hero: 51 starts for 37 wins and five places, incorporating most of Australia's major races, including the 1930 Melbourne Cup. In 1932, Phar Lap also won America's richest race, the US$50 000 Agua Caliente, against some of the world's greatest horses.

It was not for this reason alone that he became legendary. Phar Lap's rise to fame coincided with the onset of the Great Depression, when people were looking for heroes and symbols of hope. When he died suddenly in the United States after the Agua Caliente win, his legend became enshrined in Australian history. Many suspected that he was the victim of foul play.

Phar Lap before the Chariot of the Sun, 1932

In 1932, after Phar Lap's death, Tasmanian artist Joseph Luke Fleury painted the large mural *Phar Lap before the Chariot of the Sun* and exhibited it at an art gallery in Sydney. He drew on the widespread hope that Phar Lap lived on in some form, depicting him in heaven surrounded by figures from classical mythology. During the exhibition, Fleury arranged for prints to be made and sold. The original has apparently not survived.

Artist – J L Fleury. Source – Museum Victoria

Phar Lap at Melbourne Museum

Donated by D J Davis and H R Telford
Photographer – John Broomfield. Source – Museum Victoria

A GENEROUS SPIRIT

Sir Macpherson Robertson, 1859–1945

Macpherson Robertson rose from poverty to become one of Australia's wealthiest men. A generous philanthropist and effective self-promoter, Robertson made his fortune from confectionery.

He began making sweets as a teenager in the bathroom of his mother's home. By the late 1920s MacRobertson's Steam Confectionery Works employed more than 2000 people. The factory complex in Fitzroy was known as 'White City', both for its white-painted buildings and white-uniformed staff. It was here that icons of Australia's confectionery were created: Old Gold, Cherry Ripe and Freddo Frog.

It is estimated that Robertson gave away £450 000 during his lifetime – then a small fortune. He supported Antarctic expeditions and gave £100 000 to create employment during the Great Depression, resulting in a new Herbarium, MacRobertson Girls' High School and a bridge over the Yarra River at Burnley.

One of his most dramatic initiatives was the 1934 centenary air race between England and Australia. The race covered more than 19 countries and 18 240 kilometres. Twenty aeroplanes competed for prizes including £10 000 and a gold cup. Public interest was immense, and large crowds gathered wherever the planes landed and took off.

Nine aeroplanes finished within the allowed 16 days. The winners, English team C W A Scott and T Campbell Black, took just under three days.

The race demonstrated the close links between Australia and the United Kingdom and raised Melbourne's profile. It also made MacRobertson a household name around the world.

Sir Macpherson Robertson, early 20th century (detail)

Source – State Library of Victoria

Centenary air race poster, 1934

Artist – Percy Trompf. Copyright – Percy Trompf Artistic Trust courtesy Josef Lebovic Gallery. Source – State Library of Victoria

A DEDICATED LIFE

Margaret Tucker ('Lilardia'), 1904–1996

Margaret Tucker was born at the Warrangesda Mission in New South Wales. Like many other Aboriginal people, she came to Melbourne seeking work during the Depression and settled in Fitzroy.

After her husband enlisted in the armed forces, Margaret Tucker went to work at Kinnears Rope Works in Footscray, which supplied weapons, rope and twine to the Allied forces in the Pacific.

A talented singer and musician, Margaret Tucker was in a group that entertained sick servicemen at the Heidelberg military hospital. She recalled: 'We loved doing that, and would shed tears when we would go the next time only to find a bed empty, where a friendly lad had passed on'.

Margaret Tucker was politically active and a co-founder of the Australian Aborigines' League in 1932. Later, she was the first Aboriginal woman appointed to the state's Aborigines Welfare Board and Ministry of Aboriginal Affairs.

Margaret Tucker performing at a concert, about 1941

Source - *Pix*, 1941

Margaret Tucker at work in a factory, 1941

Source - *Pix*, 1941

A CHILD'S WAR

Life in wartime Melbourne was very different to peacetime Melbourne for children as well as adults. Fathers were away fighting 'Mr Hitler', while many mothers worked long hours in offices and factories. Food and petrol were rationed, making days out a rarity. Children helped grow vegetables in backyard 'victory gardens'. Trenches were dug across school playgrounds, with air-raid drills held weekly. For several weeks in 1942, when fears of invasion heightened, some city children were evacuated to rural areas.

But wartime could be exciting, too. Military marches through the city streets, fireside games of strategy and battleships, and heroic tales of soldiers in far-off lands all lit the imagination of Melbourne children, distracting them from some of the fears and losses of the war.

World War Two soldier is welcomed home, 1940s

Source – State Library of Victoria

Board game, 'The Bombadier', Paul Bruce and Co., Brunswick, about 1939

This simple game of aim and shoot was optimistically described as 'skilful, fascinating and amusing'.

Donated by Kerry Smith. Photographer – Rodney Start. Source – Museum Victoria

79

SUPPORTING THE NEEDY

For some, life had always been a struggle, and the Great Depression only made things worse. Children were among those who suffered most. Child Endowment payments would not be introduced until 1941. In the absence of government support, Melburnians' charitable efforts often focused on children from poor or fatherless families.

Pregnant women who were unmarried or already had many children were often desperate. Some had illegal and dangerous 'backyard' abortions; others abandoned their babies. Unmarried mothers were pressured to surrender their babies for adoption, while neglected and ill-treated children were removed from their parents by government officials.

The Methodist Babies' Home in South Yarra was one of many institutions established to care for children until adoptive parents could be found. Oswald Barnett, a campaigner for slum clearances and public housing, founded the home in 1929.

Babies' bottles in sterilising rack, about 1929

There were not enough nurses to hold the babies as they were fed, so bottles of milk were held in place by chaff-filled pillows as the babies sucked.

Donated by Copelen Street Family Services. Photographer – Rodney Start. Source – Museum Victoria

Washing babies at the Methodist Babies' Home

Source – Uniting Church of Australia, Synod of Victoria, Archives

HECLA ELECTRICS

Local manufacturer Hecla Electrics became a household name in Melbourne during the 1920s. Clarence Marriott registered the Hecla brand name and logo in 1918. It was inspired by the recent eruption of Iceland's volcano Mt Heckla.

Clarence Marriott and his father, James, were metal workers who had made Australia's first carbon filament electric radiators in 1899, and also built an early steam car. As electricity use exploded, they began producing a range of popular appliances for domestic and commercial use.

In 1927, the company shifted from small premises in the central city to a bigger, electric-powered factory in South Yarra.

Hecla ceased manufacturing in Melbourne in the 1980s.

Hecla kettles, 1920s–30s

Photographer – Rodney Start. Source – Museum Victoria

Brochure, 'Hecla Electrical Appliances'

On loan from Marriott family

SUBURBAN CITY   1945–1980

On a cool, breezy Sunday in December 1947, a small group of people gathered on the pier at Port Melbourne. Among them was Arthur Calwell, Australia's first minister for immigration.

They awaited the HMAS *Kanimbla*, a troop ship bringing to Melbourne the first 'displaced persons' from war-torn Europe. A train waited alongside the ship, destined for the newly opened Bonegilla Migrant Reception Centre.

Within two decades, almost one million immigrants had disembarked in Melbourne, from countries as diverse as Britain, Latvia, Italy and Greece. The city's cultural transformation had begun.

KEY DATES

1945 Melbourne's population: **1 180 200**

1945 World War Two ends

1948 First Holden car rolls off the production line at Port Melbourne

1954 Royal visit by Queen Elizabeth II, the first by a reigning monarch

1956 Melbourne hosts the XVI Olympic Games

1956 Television transmission begins in Melbourne

1960 Chadstone, Melbourne's first suburban shopping mall, opens

1967 Ronald Ryan is hanged at Pentridge Prison, the last man to be legally executed in Australia

1970 70 000 people march in protest against the Vietnam War

1970 Melbourne's international airport opens at Tullamarine

1977 Last ocean liner carrying assisted immigrants docks in Melbourne

1978 West Gate Bridge opens

1980 Melbourne's population: **2 787 400**

Melbourne changed dramatically in the years after World War Two. The city stretched outwards and upwards in the postwar decades to meet the demand for housing and industry. Construction had slowed during the war years, and now migrants and new families needed homes.

Melbourne had embraced new town planning ideals emerging from America in the early 20th century. The 1929 'Plan for General Development' established the first framework for Melbourne's development, creating zoned land use and reserves for future parklands and roads. After World War Two the Melbourne and Metropolitan Board of Works took on responsibility for planning the city's future growth. Its 1954 'Melbourne Metropolitan Planning Scheme' shaped the next three decades of transformation.

Rural zones, or 'green wedges', were established to limit the city's sprawl, and decentralised business and industrial centres were proposed to concentrate commercial activities such as retail development. Twenty-eight major arterial roads were planned, extending radially from the CBD and through the existing built-up areas.

Construction of Melbourne's first true 'freeway', the South Eastern Freeway (now the Monash Freeway), began in 1961, followed by the Tullamarine Freeway in 1969 and the Eastern Freeway in 1971.

Long-standing road problems were also addressed. Since the earliest years of settlement, the difficulty of crossing the lower Yarra and Maribyrnong Rivers had hindered development of Melbourne's western suburbs. Finally, in 1968, construction began on a modern high-level bridge with sufficient clearance for shipping. On 15 October 1970, Melbourne made world headlines when a partially constructed span of the West Gate Bridge collapsed, killing 35 construction workers. It was Australia's worst industrial accident. After a royal commission, detailed design review and strengthening, the bridge finally opened on 15 November 1978.

In the central city, the landscape was changing dramatically too. Skyscrapers broke the old 132-foot (40-metre) height limit, and streetscapes began to modernise. In the name of progress, old Melbourne was fast disappearing. Some called for greater controls on development and fought to save the city's finest heritage from Whelan the Wrecker's demolition ball.

Bourke Street, Melbourne, about 1956

Source – National Archives of Australia

85

Atherton Street, Fitzroy, looking south from Webb Street towards Gertrude Street, late 1950s

This street vanished when the Atherton Gardens Housing Commission high-rise estate was built.

Photographer – J L O'Brien. Source – University of Melbourne Archives

West Gate Bridge, 1979

Since its completion in 1978, the bridge has become one of Melbourne's most prominent landmarks, snaking across the mudflats of the lower Yarra.

Photographer – Wolfgang Sievers. Source – National Library of Australia

Others questioned the scale and shape of Melbourne's future and its impact on the environment.

But development continued. Entire inner-suburban neighbourhoods were bulldozed by the Housing Commission of Victoria between 1960 and the mid-1970s to construct high-rise apartment towers. The Housing Commission had been established in 1938, following a campaign by social reformer Oswald Barnett that highlighted the poverty and living conditions in parts of the inner suburbs. After World War Two, the Housing Commission built estates for low-income families on the inner-city fringes of Melbourne, using innovative construction techniques with precast concrete. Run-down neighbourhoods in suburbs such as Fitzroy, Carlton and South Melbourne were demolished, and replaced by 45 high-rise towers. Critics argued that 'suburbs in the sky' were hardly an improvement on the neighbourhoods they replaced. Community resistance to further clearances in the 1970s brought an end to the high-rise program.

Melbourne's outer fringes were changing dramatically too. A prosperous economy and full employment made the suburban dream affordable for many. Orchards and paddocks gave way to thousands of new homes, bursting with young families. Some were constructed, room by room, by struggling owner-builders; others were built *en masse* in estate developments by commercial developers such as A V Jennings. Car ownership quadrupled, filling the new roads and shopping mall car parks. By 1960, the suburban sprawl had extended to Broadmeadows, Nunawading and Frankston.

Both government and commercial interests fed the suburban dream. After World War Two, women were largely pushed out of the workforce into 'traditional' occupations, which generally focused on the home, ensuring that men were again the family breadwinners. At the same time, a proliferation of new products and technologies became available for the home, advertised through magazines and the new medium of television, launched in 1956. Tight moral boundaries were wrapped around the modern suburban home, too, defining the behaviour of the nuclear family.

Life for the suburban pioneers wasn't perfect. Arriving at the dream home in a brand-new suburb, a family might find no bitumen roads, footpaths, sewerage, schools or shops. Yet the challenges of living on the suburban frontier could help cement new communities together.

LUXURY PASSAGE TO MELBOURNE

The *Orcades* was the first purpose-built ocean liner to enter the England–Australia passenger trade after World War Two. She was built in north-west England for the Orient Steam Navigation Company. The *Orcades* set new standards in style and passenger comfort, accommodating some 1542 passengers in first and tourist classes.

With a top speed of 25 knots, the *Orcades* was then the largest and fastest passenger ship on the Australian route. Her maiden voyage to Melbourne in January 1949 took just 28 days, cutting 10 days off the pre-war record. She brought out many immigrants and later became a cruise liner.

The *Orcades* made 55 voyages to Australia. She is remembered in Melbourne for her service as a floating hotel during the 1956 Olympic Games.

She was broken up in 1973.

Australia Ahead, immigration booklet, about 1950
Source – Museum Victoria

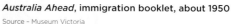

Orcades model, 1:48 scale

On loan from P & O Heritage Collection, courtesy Queenscliffe Maritime Museum
Photographer – Jon Augier

Immigrants disembarking from the *Zuiderkruis* in Melbourne, December 1954

Source – National Archives of Australia

The pressures for social change in Melbourne were building as diversity wove bright threads through the fabric of Melbourne life. On the streets, in homes and in schools, immigrants introduced new clothing styles, culinary traditions and customs.

Foods rarely seen in Melbourne 20 years earlier revolutionised dining and shopping habits all over the city. Cafes, restaurants and shops in Lygon Street (Carlton), Sydney Road (Brunswick) and Acland Street (St Kilda) became places where old and new Melbourne met.

Butchers and tailors, greengrocers, restaurants and fish-and-chip shops – all these businesses had been the mainstay of countless Melbourne families, and now postwar migrants embraced the opportunity to run them. They could get a start without large amounts of capital, special skills or English proficiency. These enterprises not only provided work for extended families, but also gave service and character to neighbourhoods.

By the 1970s, supermarkets were starting to compete with the local specialist stores, while food production was shifting to light-industrial precincts on Melbourne's outskirts. Milk bars and family-run factories, once such a feature of Melbourne's inner suburbs, would soon be few and far between.

Another important part of Melbourne life had changed far less: the tradition of Saturday afternoon football. In 1963, Melbourne football attendances hit record levels, averaging more than 150 000 diehard fans each week. Inner-suburban footy grounds were the game's tribal heartlands, with only 13 matches a year played at the Melbourne Cricket Ground. On Saturday afternoons supporters headed for Arden Street (North Melbourne), Victoria Park (Collingwood), Glenferrie Oval (Hawthorn) and other grounds, criss-crossing Melbourne on trains, trams, foot and by car. Each ground had its own character and notoriety, but by modern standards, they were no-frills – wooden benches and standing-room terraces, exposed to the wind and rain.

Postwar migrants in the inner suburbs adopted the game with a passion. At the same time, football's traditional supporters were moving to the new outer suburbs. In a few short years the Victorian Football League would face a revolution as old grounds closed, the game nationalised and some Victorian teams moved interstate.

Life in the suburbs, Croydon, 1970

Photographer – Laurie Richards. Copyright – Commonwealth Bank of Australia
Source – Museum Victoria

In 1975, International Women's Day was celebrated with a spirited march along Bourke Street, ending at Carlton Gardens

Source – National Archives of Australia

Other changes were also brewing in Melbourne. By the 1960s and 1970s, a new generation began to look beyond the suburban dream of lawnmower, Laminex kitchen and car in the driveway. Melbourne's once unfashionable and poor inner suburbs became the focus of experimental ways of living. Community gardens, arts and theatre, political protest – all sorts of social activism flourished there.

Melburnians increasingly took their dissent to the streets and raised their voices on issues such as Australia's military involvement in the Vietnam War, the construction of the new Eastern Freeway, and gay and women's rights. Not all the crowds on Melbourne's streets were demonstrating, though; some were celebrating, others commemorating. Royal and presidential visits and a stream of overseas celebrities brought crowds out onto the streets. Among Melbourne's most enduring street events are the Anzac Day march, held since 1916, and the Moomba parade, which has made its way down Swanston Street each Labour Day since 1955.

The rise of youth culture in the later 1960s was reflected in Melbourne's flourishing local music scene and the Sunbury rock festivals. After years of imitating British and American groups, local musicians were creating a distinctly

Australian form of urban music in suburban garages and crowded inner-city pubs. And audiences were loving it.

The success of the Sunbury festivals proved there was a market for original local rock music. Bands such as Skyhooks, which shot to prominence on the hit ABC-TV show 'Countdown', explored life in their own city and its suburbs – 'Balwyn Calling', 'Carlton (Lygon Street Limbo)', 'Toorak Cowboys' – rather than singing about London or California.

Melbourne was finding a new identity.

PROTESTING VIETNAM

'The biggest crowd I've ever seen,' was how US President Lyndon Baines Johnson described Melburnians' response to his visit in 1966. It may also have been the most colourful.

Johnson was in Australia at the invitation of Prime Minister Harold Holt, who had proclaimed that Australia would go 'All the way with LBJ' in its support of the United States in the Vietnam War.

On 21 October, in South Yarra, the president's limousine was pelted with red and green paint-bombs by anti-war protesters. This shirt belonged to one of the president's security men – among them Rufus Youngblood, who had also been in President Kennedy's entourage at the time of his assassination.

The protestors were charged, and their defending barrister apologetically wrote to Johnson that they had been 'excited to fever pitch by your presence and the consequent air of exultation and triumph'.

Paint-splattered shirt worn by Johnson's security guard, 1966

Photographer – Benjamin Healley. Source – Museum Victoria

President Lyndon B Johnson in a paint-splattered car, with Rufus Youngblood alongside, 1966

Source – Fairfax Photos

Protest badges, about 1970

On 8 May 1970, some 70 000 people marched through Melbourne demanding that Australian troops be brought home from Vietnam. Badges and leaflets publicised their cause.

Donated by Nic Maclellan, Ken Norling and Michael Hamel-Green
Photographer – Benjamin Healley. Source – Museum Victoria

COLLECTING FOR A GLORY BOX

Kath Davis, 1921–

Kath Davis moved from country Victoria to Lilydale in Melbourne's outer east as a newlywed in 1944. It was another 10 years before she and her husband could buy their three-bedroom brick home in Main Street, Lilydale.

In preparing her glory box, Kath Davis had chosen attractive items that she would be unlikely to acquire after marriage, when purchases would be limited to the practical. A skilled needlewoman, she produced a fine collection of fancywork for her future home.

A glory box was a collection of objects, compiled by a young woman through careful saving and needlecraft, in preparation for married life. The interior of many a couple's first home owed much to the contents of a glory box.

Kath Davis on her daughter Wendy's christening day, 8 January 1950

Source – Kath Davis

Treasures from Kath Davis's glory box

Donated by Kath Davis.
Photographer – Benjamin Healley

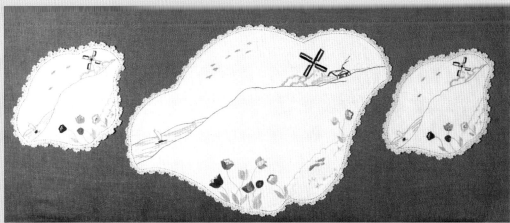

SELLING RAVIOLI TO MELBOURNE

Small businesses have been the mainstay of many immigrant families.

Nello and Bruna Borghesi opened La Tosca Food Processing in 1947. They first manufactured pasta sauce and tinned vegetables. However, their small enterprise could not compete with the larger mass-production companies.

Nello Borghesi decided to give handmade pasta a try. The ravioli roller pictured here was used during the early 1950s to stamp the pasta dough and create the pockets for the ravioli filling, which was spread over the pasta with a spatula. Ravioli was delivered in the family van to delis and restaurants in Carlton, the northern suburbs and the city. The exclusive Florentino's and Mario's restaurants were La Tosca customers.

As Melbourne became more cosmopolitan and demand grew, La Tosca moved to machine production and developed an entire range of pasta. The business continues to operate to this day.

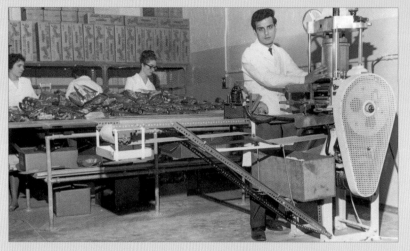

Lionello (Lio) Borghesi – Nello and Bruna's son – operating the ravioli machine that he constructed himself, at the La Tosca factory, about 1969

Source – Italian Historical Society CO.AS.IT and Borghesi family

Ravioli roller and pasta cutters

On loan from La Tosca Pasta and Borghesi family
Photographer – Benjamin Healley. Source – Museum Victoria

SATURDAY ARVO FEVER

The 1960s were glory years for Essendon Football Club, which won the premiership in 1962 and 1965. Supporters spent many Saturdays at Windy Hill cheering behind the goals in the red and black team colours.

For the avid footy fan, watching the game just wasn't enough. Mothers and grandmothers knitted scarves and jumpers in team colours, fans pored over footy cards, fixtures and magazines, and manufacturers produced souvenirs, including football-shaped money boxes and tea towels.

Football barrackers at the Melbourne Cricket Ground, 1960s

Photographer – Mal Thomson. Source – Peter Thomson

Essendon tea towel

On loan from Essendon Hall of Fame
Photographer – Jon Augier. Source – Museum Victoria

Essendon money box, 1960s

On loan from Essendon Hall of Fame
Photographer – Jon Augier. Source – Museum Victoria

CHANGING CITY 1980-PRESENT

It was supposed to be a massive copper spire tipped with gold, soaring over a huge new cultural complex. But when Melbourne's Arts Centre opened in 1984, eyes turned proudly to the modest latticework frame that would become a symbol of Melbourne.

Its opening heralded a new era of Melbourne as a cultural and events capital.

KEY DATES

1980 MELBOURNE'S POPULATION: 2 787 400

1982 MELBOURNE CONCERT HALL (NOW HAMER HALL) OPENS

1983 A MASSIVE DUST STORM HITS MELBOURNE, FOLLOWED BY 'ASH WEDNESDAY' BUSHFIRES

1986 A CAR BOMB EXPLODES OUTSIDE RUSSELL STREET POLICE HEADQUARTERS

1987 MASS SHOOTINGS IN HODDLE STREET AND QUEEN STREET

1992 MELBOURNE'S MAIN STREET, SWANSTON STREET, IS CLOSED TO THROUGH TRAFFIC

1996 AUSTRALIAN FORMULA ONE GRAND PRIX AT ALBERT PARK BEGINS

1996 CONSTRUCTION BEGINS ON THE CITYLINK TOLLWAY, INCLUDING THE BOLTE BRIDGE AND TWO TUNNELS BENEATH THE YARRA RIVER

1998 VICTORIANS ARE WITHOUT GAS FOR TWO WEEKS AFTER AN EXPLOSION AT THE ESSO LONGFORD GAS PLANT IN GIPPSLAND

2000 MELBOURNE MUSEUM OPENS

2002 'MELBOURNE 2030' PLAN IS INTRODUCED TO SHAPE AND CONCENTRATE GROWTH

2004 ROYAL EXHIBITION BUILDING RECEIVES WORLD HERITAGE LISTING

2006 MELBOURNE HOSTS THE COMMONWEALTH GAMES

Melbourne in 1980 was on the cusp of an extraordinary period of change. In the space of two decades, it would be transformed by deindustrialisation, high-density housing construction, reforms to licensing laws and the staging of major sporting and cultural events.

The impact of Melbourne's growth could be seen in both the inner city and the outer suburbs. Land on the urban fringes was subdivided to form suburbs such as Patterson Lakes to the south-east, built around a series of waterways developed in the 1970s from remnants of the Carrum Swamp. Nearby, the suburbs of Berwick and Cranbourne began to develop, while Werribee and Sydenham in the west and Epping and Craigieburn to the north of Melbourne rang with the sounds of saws and nail guns in the 1980s and 1990s.

Since 2000, Melbourne's northern suburbs have expanded rapidly at Taylors Lakes, Roxburgh Park and Caroline Springs. In 2003, work began north of the city in Aurora, touted as Melbourne's first environmentally sustainable suburb, featuring water and waste recycling, green-efficient appliances, greater solar energy use and improved access to public transport.

Melbourne's population has become the fastest growing of any Australian city, expanding at the same rate as during the immigration boom of the 1950s and 1960s. By mid-2006, the city's population was almost 3.75 million.

In many ways, Melbourne has become an archetypal modern city, with large suburban shopping centres servicing distant suburbs and customers who are largely car-dependent. Chadstone Shopping Centre, the first freestanding regional shopping centre in Melbourne, opened in the city's south-east in 1960. It has become Australia's largest shopping centre, covering about 132 000 square metres, and is still expanding. As more shopping centres opened, they challenged long-established shopping strips. In areas such as Dandenong, shopping centres have drained the economic blood from shopping strips, but streets such as Sydney Road in Brunswick and Koornang Road in Carnegie have endured as economic and social hubs for their communities.

Even as the suburbs have grown and changed, the 'Melbourne 2030' plan has tempered development in Melbourne. Released in 2002, it aims to reduce the number of new dwellings in rural areas, limit dispersed development and increase the density of existing areas of Melbourne.

Aerial view of St Kilda Road, Melbourne, 1994
Source – National Archives of Australia

Docklands development, 2006

Photographer – Craig Abraham. Source – Fairfaxphotos

Building the city's underground rail loop, 1977

Photographer – Wolfgang Sievers. Source – State Library of Victoria

It has met with forceful opposition from communities in established suburbs such as Camberwell, where the prospect of increased density and modern architectural forms is seen to threaten the historic character of the suburb.

Down by the Yarra River in the inner city, the vision 'Melbourne 2030' championed was already being realised. The transformation of the industrial southern banks into Southgate began in the 1980s and 1990s, incorporating a major casino, apartments and restaurants. The city has increasingly turned to face the river. Further downstream it has turned to face the salt water at Docklands. Here, three kilometres of river frontage and 200 hectares of land and water have been developed from industrial and transport use into a series of interlinked precincts, combining high-rise residential apartments and commercial buildings.

The trend to re use sites had begun in the 1980s in other areas, too. The Vickers-Ruwolt factory site in Burnley, in Melbourne's inner east, was one of Australia's largest and best-equipped heavy engineering works. By World War Two, when the business reorganised to manufacture armaments, it covered eight hectares and employed 2000 workers. The site was sold in the late 1980s and developed into Victoria Gardens, a major complex that includes a shopping centre, offices and homes. The site shows few signs of its former use.

The revival of areas such as Port Melbourne has been less drastic, with factories and warehouses being cleared or converted into higher density, higher income apartments, jostling for glimpses of Port Phillip Bay.

As Melbourne has grown and changed, the landscape in which it sits has appeared to recede. Backyards have disappeared under subdivisions or large extensions. The 'green belts' lauded in the 1970s, in areas such as Eltham on the city's northern fringe, have been increasingly urbanised, and sections of inner urban parkland have been overtaken by sporting venues.

The National Tennis Centre opened in parkland near the Yarra in 1988, replacing Kooyong as the city's main tennis venue and providing a site for the annual Australian Open Tennis Championship. Further sporting venues were soon opened in the same area, later to host the Melbourne 2006 Commonwealth Games. To further limit the effect of lost space in Melbourne, 'green wedges' of open land were included in the 'Melbourne 2030' strategy. Some of the lost space in the inner city was replaced with new parks such as Birrarung Marr, built on eight hectares of land from the former Jolimont Railway Yards and planted with native flora.

A WATER SMART HOME

This home is an elegant example of how measures to reduce water and carbon emissions can be built into Melbourne's suburban lifestyle. This custom-built home is passive solar in design and completely self-sufficient in water.

Lorraine Hughes's home incorporates a rainwater harvesting and greywater recycling system. This system collects wastewater from the bathroom and laundry, passes it through a peat filtration system and stores it in an underground tank. The greywater is used for flushing toilets and watering her drought-tolerant garden.

In line with regulations, Lorraine Hughes uses lilac-coloured hoses in her garden to indicate that greywater is in use. She wanted to install similarly coloured taps to greywater outlets. Lorraine was unable to locate a retail source for lilac taps, as community and legislative needs had out-paced retail supply. Lorraine decided to paint the taps herself.

Lorraine's house has been featured as part of the Water Smart Home Project, a community-based project funded by the Smart Water Fund and developed by Museum Victoria.

Lorraine Hughes outside her home, 2007

Photographer – Rodney Start. Source – Museum Victoria

Greywater tap, 2007

Donated by Lorraine Hughes
Photographer – Rodney Start. Source – Museum Victoria

Aerial view of Scienceworks
Photographer – David Loram. Source – Museum Victoria

As Melbourne's position as a sporting events capital was reinforced, other areas were converted into sports venues. Some are used for major annual events, such as the Australian Formula One Grand Prix, which since 1996 has been run on the route of an earlier racetrack around Albert Park lake. The race attracted vocal criticism from local residents concerned about the noise, crowds and disruption to local birdlife, but has proved a popular attraction for Melburnians and tourists alike. Like many international sporting events, however, its future presence in Melbourne is not guaranteed.

Since the 1980s, Melbourne's more traditional sports have changed too. In 1982, the first of the Victorian football clubs, South Melbourne, was transferred to Sydney to become the Sydney Swans. It was the first move towards national expansion of Victoria's beloved game. Many local supporters felt alienated, but all the Melbourne clubs retained a local base and following. Melbourne still remains the spiritual heart of Australian Rules football.

Progress also swept through Melbourne's cultural venues. Museum Victoria opened the first of its new venues, Scienceworks, at the old Spotswood Pumping Station in 1992, and six years later opened the Immigration Museum in the old Customs House in Flinders Street. In 2000, Melbourne Museum opened – the flagship venue for Museum Victoria. The National Gallery of Victoria also underwent redevelopment. It opened a second venue in 2002, focusing on its Australian collection at the newly developed Federation Square, where much-maligned high-rise office buildings along the Yarra River were replaced with a public square and cultural precinct.

Increasing numbers of settlers from Asia, Africa and the Middle East arrived into this evolving landscape of the 1980s and 1990s. Many of these settlers were foreign students, family reunion immigrants and refugees. But Melbourne's largest immigrant community remains the England-born, followed by communities from Greece, Vietnam and New Zealand. Three-quarters of Victorians live in Melbourne, and this proportion continues to grow in Melbourne's favour.

Hand-in-hand with the cultural development of the city has come a culinary transformation. Melburnians welcomed new cafes into their city and suburbs, with tables spilling on to the pavements and menus rich with foods from around the world. From the food halls of Queen Victoria Market to the fine-dining restaurants lining Southbank, Melburnians have been discovering the social and economic benefits of the city's culinary bounty.

103

MELBOURNE LANEWAYS

In the lanes and alleys of the central city, Melbourne has developed a distinctive character over the past two decades, as tiny cafes jostle for space with restaurants and boutique shops. The laneways and alleys are an unwitting result of Robert Hoddle's original grid for the city, drawn up in 1837. Between each of the major streets Governor Bourke insisted Hoddle add narrow streets for service access. These were eventually intersected with laneways that were smaller still – eventually the ideal place for modern small businesses.

Changes to retail laws have meant that cafes can now place tables on the pavements, encouraging outdoor eating, and relaxed licensing laws have extended the hours and places that alcohol can be consumed.

Degraves Street, Melbourne, 2008

Photographer – Jon Augier. Source – Museum Victoria

Smoke plume rising from the Coode Island chemical fire, 1991

Melbourne has also embraced other forms of diversity. When Aboriginal footballer Nicky Winmar raised his jumper to point to his skin in defiance at racial abuse, it marked an important moment for both self-determination and the fight against racism in sport.

Legislative changes enshrined new cultural attitudes in Melbourne and in Victoria. In 1980, homosexuality was finally decriminalised in Victoria, after years of community activism. In 1995, Victoria's *Equal Opportunity Act* outlined broad grounds for unlawful discrimination, and in 2001 the *Racial and Religious Tolerance Act* enshrined racial and religious tolerance.

Other types of political change have occurred too. During the mid-1990s, 210 local councils across Victoria were replaced with 78 larger councils. Management of public utilities such as the train and tram networks were put into private hands. And law and order problems were raising doubts about the efficacy of policing and social policy.

The year 1986 marked the start of a painful period in Melbourne's criminal history. That year, the Russell Street Police Headquarters was bombed by criminals as a diversion from a distant robbery. The force of the car bomb blew in every window in the building and killed a police officer. It was Melbourne's first act of criminal bombing. Little over a year later, in August 1987, the city faced the first of two mass murders, random acts by gunmen in Hoddle Street, Clifton Hill, and Queen Street in the city. These crimes shook confidence in Melbourne as a safe city. That confidence was further shaken with a series of murders within the criminal fraternity from the late 1990s, dubbed the 'gangland murders'. Yet by international standards Melbourne's crime rate has remained low.

Massive infrastructure projects have also occupied the government. Melbourne's first underground rail loop was completed in 1981. It had been a long journey, beginning in 1929 when the Metropolitan Town Planning Commission recommended that railway lines be built under the northern and eastern sides of the central business district. Four decades later, after years of discussion and costly delays, work finally began. Four massive tunnels under the city, running for a total of 13 kilometres, and three new stations were built between 1971 and 1985, with sections opening progressively.

The development of infrastructure in Melbourne was not only a story of triumph, however. In August 1991, Melbourne's skies darkened with smoke from a huge chemical fire on Coode Island, an island between the Yarra and Maribyrnong Rivers. Coode Island had been created when a shipping canal was constructed in 1886, and was used for bulk storage of petrochemicals.

105

A MIGRANT'S STORY

Nyabana Riek, 1977–

All that Nyabana Riek has as mementoes of her home can be held in two hands. They are precious ties to her family, culture and Africa.

Nyabana was born in 1977 in southern Sudan. When she was nine years old Nyabana and her sister Mary were sent by their parents to Ethiopia to escape the war. After seven years of living in refugee camps, they made the dangerous trek across the mountains to Kenya, where they applied to join Mary's husband in Australia. It took three long years to be accepted. Nyabana arrived in Melbourne in 1995 with no English and no friends. She is now an Australian citizen and has made Australia her home, along with many refugees from southern Sudan.

Nyabana brought with her this string of four beads, the poignant remains of a childhood necklace from southern Sudan. She bought the earrings in Nairobi, Kenya, just before she left for Australia. Her other few possessions included a Bible and hymnbook published in her Nuer language.

Nyabana Riek's beads and earrings

Donated by Nyabana Riek
Photographer – Rodney Start. Source – Museum Victoria

Nyabana Riek, late 1990s

Source – Nyabana Riek

Aerial view of Melbourne's skyline with Melbourne Museum and the Royal Exhibition Building in the foreground, 2000

Photographer – Andrew Chapman. Source – Museum Victoria

The fire cast a large pall of smoke over the city, and city workers were asked to remain indoors to avoid the toxic fumes. The fire burned for two days and destroyed more than two-thirds of the storage tanks on the island. In 2000, Coode Island was re-confirmed as Victoria's major petro-chemical storage facility – an alternative site could not be found.

In September 1998, an explosion and fire at the Longford gas facility in south-eastern Victoria took the lives of two workers and injured eight more. It halted gas supplies for two weeks to Melbourne, as well as the rest of the state and parts of New South Wales and South Australia, affecting more than one million households and businesses reliant on gas for cooking, heating and hot water.

Melbourne had already faced disaster on several occasions in recent times. On 8 February 1983, a huge cloud of dust descended on Melbourne. The dust was topsoil from the Mallee and Wimmera regions in Victoria's north-west, loosened by years of vegetation removal and dried by an El Niño weather pattern. A cold front swept the state on that stiflingly hot day, whipping up 50 000 tons of soil into a cloud 320 metres thick. When the cloud struck the city the sky turned black, and the winds that came with it unroofed dozens of houses. The effect on the city was dramatic, but worse for farmers.

The loss of topsoil, combined with the drought, would take years to overcome.

Just one week after the dust came, Melbourne's skies again darkened as nearly 200 fires erupted in south-eastern Australia, including devastating fires on Melbourne's fringes. 'Ash Wednesday' saw a greater loss of life than any other bushfire in Australian history, claiming 47 lives in Victoria alone. It was tragically surpassed by the Black Saturday fires of 7 February 2009, in which 173 Victorians died, 78 communities were impacted, and 430,000 hectares of land destroyed.

These events cast a shadow over Melbourne for years to come, making Melburnians acutely conscious of the connection between their city and its environment. Future challenges that come with a growing population – such as water shortages, the loss of open space and the provision of road and rail services – are those faced by most modern cities.

But for Melbourne, named one of the world's most liveable cities, the question is even more urgent: how can the city retain its cultural richness, diversity, safety, affordability, accessibility and economic vibrancy into the future?

AN AUSTRALIAN FIRST

The automated DNA sequencer is one of the most important developments in the history of biotechnology. This machine, an Applied Biosystems ABI 370, was the first automated sequencer in Australia, purchased in 1987–88 by The Walter and Eliza Hall Institute, Parkville, for the Australian Genome Research Facility. It facilitates the rapid analysis of genes, and the technology has enabled the human genome to be sequenced. Prior to the automated DNA sequencer, genetic analysis was achieved through a laborious manual method, using radioisotopes.

Australia's first automated DNA sequencer provided a vital boost to the development of a vaccine against one of the major diseases of the world, malaria. The sequencer was used until 2001, when it was superseded by a more advanced model. Work continues towards a malaria vaccine.

Australia's first DNA sequencer (detail)

Donated by Australian Genome Research Facility of the
Walter and Eliza Hall Institute
Photographer – Rodney Start. Source – Museum Victoria

MELBOURNE 2006 COMMONWEALTH GAMES

In 2006, Melbourne hosted the Commonwealth Games. Millions of viewers from around the Commonwealth tuned in to watch the 4500 international athletes compete in Melbourne. The Melbourne Cricket Ground hosted athletics competitions, the start and finish of the marathon, and the opening and closing ceremonies, featuring the largest fireworks display ever seen in the city. Events were also held at Melbourne Park, Olympic Park and Telstra Dome, and suburban and regional sites. Melbourne's notoriously inclement weather even held out for the entire 12 days of competition.

The tram 'flying' into the MCG during the opening ceremony

Source – Fairfaxphotos

The Queen's baton

Donated by Melbourne 2006 Commonwealth Games Corporation
Photographer – Jon Augier. Source – Museum Victoria

The flying tram

The flying tram was the centrepiece of the Melbourne 2006 Commonwealth Games' opening ceremony. The idea of a flying tram came from Fremantle-based designer and artist Andrew Carter. The tram was made by Plumb Engineering.

During the opening ceremony, the tram flew in on a steel cable. Its floor opened to allow 120 performers to step up through a hole in the stage and leave through the doors of the tram.

The Queen's baton

Since 1958, the Queen's Baton Relay has been the traditional curtain raiser to the Commonwealth Games. On 14 March 2005, Her Majesty placed a digital message in the baton at Buckingham Palace, signalling the start of a journey across the 71 nations of the Commonwealth. The baton was designed and manufactured by Melbourne-based Charlwood Design Pty Ltd, supported by 23 other Australian companies.

The baton harnesses advanced technology, including a global positioning system, cameras and 200 light-emitting diodes triggered by the runners.

ACKNOWLEDGEMENTS

CONTRIBUTING AUTHORS

Melbourne: a city of stories was developed as a companion text to the Museum Victoria exhibition *The Melbourne Story*, which opened at Melbourne Museum in March 2008.

Reflecting the content of the exhibition, this book draws on the work of many curators and other experts who helped with the development of the exhibition. The authors would like to thank colleagues within Museum's History and Technology and Indigenous Cultures Departments: Carla Pascoe, Ben Thomas, Lindy Allen, Mike Green and Sandra Smith, as well as publishing and image management staff, collection managers and conservators. Particular thanks are due to Richard Gillespie, Head of History and Technology at Museum Victoria, for his contribution, guidance and support.

Warm thanks are also due to the many people beyond Museum Victoria who generously shared their expertise in support of the exhibition, including Tony Birch, Kate Darian-Smith, Graeme Davison, Meighen Katz, John Lack, Judy McKinty, Peter Marsh, Andrew May, Seamus O'Hanlon, Gary Presland, Marion Quartly and Graham Willett. Finally, the exhibition and the book would not have been possible without the generosity of the many people who shared their personal stories, including the Borghesi family, Kath Davis, Lorraine Hughes and Nyabana Riek.

The objects featured in this book are primarily drawn from Museum Victoria's collection. The images were also drawn from the museum's collection, unless otherwise noted.

The La Tosca label (p. 94) was reproduced with the permission of the Italian Historical Society.

Rebecca Carland, Curator, Sustainable Futures; Matthew Churchward, Senior Curator, Engineering & Transport; David Crotty, Curator, Engineering; Liza Dale-Hallett, Senior Curator, Sustainable Futures; David Demant, Senior Curator, Information & Communication; Richard Gillespie, Head, History & Technology Department; Fiona Kinsey, Curator, Domestic & Community Life; Moya McFadzean, Senior Curator, Migration; Michael Reason, Curator, History & Technology; Adrian Regan, Assistant Curator, History & Technology; Sarah Rood, Assistant Curator, Water Smart Home Project; Antoinette Smith, Senior Curator, Indigenous Cultures (South-eastern Australia); Charlotte Smith, Senior Curator, Public Life & Institutions; Deborah Tout-Smith, Senior Curator, Cultural Diversity; Nurin Veis, Senior Curator, Human Biology & Medicine; Elizabeth Willis, Curator Emeritus.

SELECTED READING

Annear, R. 2005, *A City Lost and Found: Whelan the Wrecker's Melbourne*, Black Inc., Melbourne.

Annear, R. 1995, *Bearbrass: imagining early Melbourne*, Mandarin, Port Melbourne.

Brown-May, A. and Swain, S. (eds) 2005, *Encyclopedia of Melbourne*, Cambridge University Press, Melbourne.

Brown-May, A. 1998, *Melbourne Street Life*, Australian Scholarly Publishing, Melbourne.

Cannon, M. 1995, rev. edn, *The Land Boomers: the complete illustrated history*, Melbourne University Press, Carlton.

Davison, G. 2004, rev. edn., *The Rise and Fall of Marvellous Melbourne*, Melbourne University Press, Carlton.

Davison, G., Dunstan, D. and McConville, C. (eds) 1985, *The Outcasts of Melbourne: essays in social history*, Allen & Unwin, Sydney.

De Serville, P. 1980, *Port Phillip Gentlemen*, Oxford University Press, Melbourne.

Goad, P. 1998, *Melbourne Architecture*, The Watermark Press, Balmain, NSW.

Museum Victoria 2006, *Melbourne's Wildlife: a field guide to fauna of Greater Melbourne*, Museum Victoria and CSIRO Publishing, Melbourne.

Serle, G. 1977, *The Golden Age: a history of the colony of Victoria 1851–1861*, Melbourne University Press, Carlton.

Shaw, A. G. L. 1996, *The History of the Port Phillip District: Victoria before Separation*, Melbourne University Press, Carlton.

Willis, E. 2003, *The Royal Exhibition Building, Melbourne: a guide*, Museum Victoria, Melbourne

INDEX

Bold entries indicate illustrated content.